WARHAMMER
AGE OF SIGMAR

From the maelstrom of a sundered world, the Eight Realms
were born. The formless and the divine exploded into life.
Strange, new worlds appeared in the firmament, each one
gilded with spirits, gods and men. Noblest of the gods was
Sigmar. For years beyond reckoning he illuminated the
realms, wreathed in light and majesty as he carved out his
reign. His strength was the power of thunder. His wisdom
was infinite. Mortal and immortal alike kneeled before his
lofty throne. Great empires rose and, for a while, treachery
was banished. Sigmar claimed the land and sky as his own
and ruled over a glorious age of myth.

But cruelty is tenacious. As had been foreseen, the great
alliance of gods and men tore itself apart. Myth and legend
crumbled into Chaos. Darkness flooded the realms. Torture,
slavery and fear replaced the glory that came before. Sigmar
turned his back on the mortal kingdoms, disgusted by their
fate. He fixed his gaze instead on the remains of the world he
had lost long ago, brooding over its charred core, searching
endlessly for a sign of hope. And then, in the dark heat of
his rage, he caught a glimpse of something magnificent. He
pictured a weapon born of the heavens. A beacon powerful
enough to pierce the endless night. An army hewn from
everything he had lost. Sigmar set his artisans to work and
for long ages they toiled, striving to harness the power of the
stars. As Sigmar's great work neared completion, he turned
back to the realms and saw that the dominion of Chaos was
almost complete. The hour for vengeance had come. Finally,
with lightning blazing across his brow, he stepped forth to
unleash his creation.

The Age of Sigmar had begun.

CONTENTS

DESIGNED BY GAMES WORKSHOP IN NOTTINGHAM

Games Workshop Ltd., Willow Road, Lenton, Nottingham, NG7 2WS, United Kingdom
Printed by Leo Paper, in China   games-workshop.com

TZEENTCH ALMIGHTY

Anarchy incarnate, the god Tzeentch is known by many titles, including the Changer of the Ways, the Master of Fortune, the Great Conspirator and the Architect of Fate. Tzeentch's domains are magic and guile, for he is the god of sorcery and deceit. Schemes, plots, and machinations are his delight.

Tzeentch is one of the Greater Chaos powers, a brother god to Khorne, Nurgle and Slaanesh, and often an ally to the pantheon's newcomer, the Great Horned Rat. Even amongst gods, Tzeentch is the undisputed master of the arcane arts, for magic is the most potent of all agents of change. This does not mean Tzeentch is above sullying his hands with war – rather that he much prefers to win battles through guile and sorcery over brute force. He favours the cunning over the strong, the manipulative over the violent. In his true shape, Tzeentch is the most outlandish of the Dark Gods. His skin crawls with constantly changing faces that leer and mock any who dare to gaze upon him. As Tzeentch speaks,

these faces appear and disappear, some repeating his words with subtle differences, or perhaps providing mocking commentary to cast doubt upon the original words. Ever shifting, nothing of Tzeentch feels definitive – even his purpose is unimaginably complex, his schemes beyond the ken of mortals. Yet Tzeentch's growing ascendancy after Sigmar's return to the Mortal Realms and the battles of the Realmgate Wars hints at plans long nursed to fruition. Embedded deep within Sigmar's grand cities, mortal cultists work in secret to advance his unknowable goals, while Tzaangor tribes raid the ancient places of the realms in search of lost treasures and esoteric knowledge. Should the need arise, Tzeentch sends his daemonic hosts forth in all their scintillating glory, to sear the land with the coruscating flames of change.

THE GREAT GAME

The never-ending struggle of each of the Chaos Gods to gain dominion over the others is known to Tzeentch as the Great Game. To the most masterful of schemers, this game offers not just endless amusement, but also boundless opportunities. Not only does Tzeentch constantly seek to further his own ambitions, but he is equally voracious in his desire to manipulate or counteract the best-laid plans of his rivals. Through convoluted machinations Tzeentch has subverted his brother gods time and again.

The Realm of Chaos is Tzeentch's playground for the Great Game. There, he instigates infighting – a pursuit of which the god never tires. One of his most infamous deeds in the Great Game was to beguile Khorne's greatest Bloodthirster, Skarbrand, into attacking his patron. It was Tzeentch's magic that crystallised the cycles of Nurgle's Garden and, although few know the full tale, it was Tzeentch's plotting that led to Slaanesh's absence. The battles for control of the Mortal Realms have only added new challenges to the Great Game.

Tzeentch's plots are manifold, but none are simple. Revelling in complication, Tzeentch's plans can appear contradictory to those few observers able to detect his influence, for he is patient and willing to wait long centuries for his obtuse intrigues to bear fruit. And Tzeentch is fickle, prone to adding elaborate intricacies to his own plots, or perhaps introducing obstacles to impede them. Indeed, the Architect of Fate rejoices in the construction of each plan as much as he revels in watching it unravel.

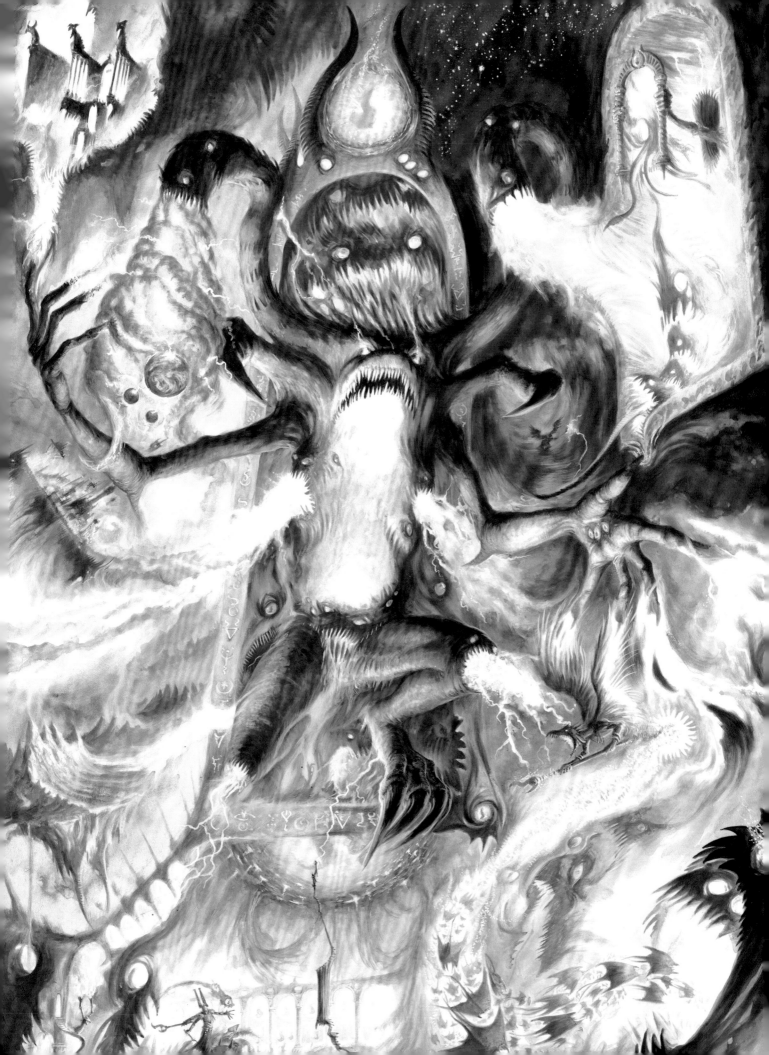

Across the realms the Lord of Sorcery spins his impossibly complex webs of secrecy, and servants long embedded in the foundations of Sigmar's realm sow the seeds of madness and fear. Where Khorne and Nurgle seek to destroy and despoil the cities of the God-King, Tzeentch plays a far longer game. In civilisation there is subtlety, complexity, mechanism and machination. Through cunning and manipulation, Tzeentch's power blossoms in this new age of reason and intrigue.

As Sigmar's followers returned to the Mortal Realms, their ranks were infiltrated. The daemon known as the Changeling used doppelgänger magic to sabotage many of the new cities of their growing civilisations. By its gilded tongue it led countless of the God-King's faithful astray. Like a spark that begins an inferno, so did the Changeling foster a hundred new cults dedicated to magic, change, knowledge and, ultimately, to Tzeentch. By its hand entire cities have already risen up in rebellion, casting down their rulers into the flames of change. Others remain outwardly loyal while heresy and sedition flow through their bloodstream like a cancer, only waiting for the right moment to strike.

The Changeling's plots had not yet reached fruition when Sigmar's agents unveiled the daemon in the twin city of Hammerhal, at the centre of a web of sorcery and lies. With warpfire and daemon hosts, the Changeling fought its way to freedom, leaving its foes in doubt and with growing suspicions – though such was its true goal all along. Now the time of change draws nearer, and the creature's twisted plans lead to a confluence of Tzeentch's triumph.

FROM THE CRYSTAL LABYRINTH

There is nothing that Tzeentch sets his iridescent eyes upon that he does not wish to seize for his own, to control and to manipulate, to change at his whim. So does the Architect of Fate sit at the centre of the Crystal Labyrinth, like a spider on a web, forever hatching plots and sending them forth.

Rivalling Khorne's domain in size, the Crystal Labyrinth's shimmering brilliance is a stark contrast to the Blood God's ruddy wastelands. Countless glittering pathways spring from the sprawling maze. Everywhere Horrors scuttle about, using their magics to grow further crystal corridors. At the heart of the Labyrinth stands the Impossible Fortress, but scattered across the tangled outer regions are nine strongholds arranged in an ever-changing hierarchy – the Fractal Fortresses. Each of these kaleidoscopic spires is home to one of the nine legions, known as convocations, that Tzeentch favours at any given time, and is ruled by its most powerful daemon. There, the titular Overseer receives commands from Tzeentch himself, in turn relaying their own version of those orders outwards to the subordinate convocations, who compete to earn their god's approval and occupy one of the fortresses. The number of convocations is in constant flux, though it is never fewer than, and is always a multiple of, nine.

Within the Realm of Chaos Tzeentch's daemons battle those of the other Dark Gods, staving off invasions or seeking to claim territory. Alliances are forged, broken, and forged again, yet none can finagle in or out of such treaties with as much skill as the minions of the Great Schemer. Tzeentch covets the Mortal Realms as well, and his forces actively pursue hundreds of different plots, such as shifting the strands of fate or covertly inveigling mortal recruits to serve in Arcanite Cults. Like their patron, the convocations seek sources of magic, spread anarchy, and corrupt ambitions. When illusion or manipulation fail, however, they resort to more direct methods, setting battlefields alight with volleys of spells and sheets of warpfire.

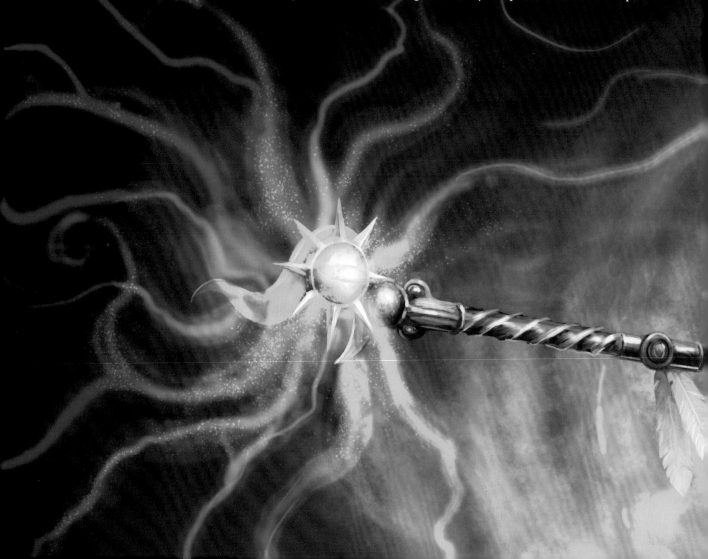

AN ETERNAL RIVALRY

Far beyond the light of sun or star, removed from all reason and reality, lies the Realm of Chaos. There, the Chaos Gods strive against one another in a never-ending power struggle. As one god grows in strength, so do the others conspire against him. Common cause will unite the disparate powers, but even then each god angles to ensure that they emerge from the alliance in a better position than the others. In the endless scheming, none of the gods fare so well as Tzeentch, and he delights in manipulating them all – tormenting ever-raging Khorne or endlessly baiting crass, melodramatic Slaanesh.

However, every Chaos God has his opposite, another whose nature is the antithesis of his own. For Tzeentch, that special foe is Nurgle. The Lord of Decay provides Tzeentch his fiercest rivalry. To Tzeentch's hope and ambition, his demand for change, Nurgle counters with opposing ideologies – a resigned despair that accepts how things are, a willingness to not just be content with the base or mundane, but to actually wallow in it. In their endless battles, Tzeentch pits his ceaseless evolution against the stagnant loop of Nurgle's closed cycle of life and death. Tzeentch, who delights in his carefully laid plans, is appalled to watch Nurgle's slovenly and indiscriminate destruction, his jovial acceptance of the natural order. The two powers never miss an opportunity to match forces against one another, be it battles over boundaries in the Realm of Chaos, expansionist wars in the Mortal Realms or even political intrigues amongst the Cities of Sigmar.

Of late, Tzeentch has gained the upper hand. In Ghyran, where once Nurgle reigned nearly unchallenged, the decaying Kingdom of Bul'ghoh was toppled due to the machinations of Kairos Fateweaver. From beside Nurgle's Great Cauldron itself the Changeling aided the Blue Scribes in stealing a seven-volume set of tomes listing cures for the Plague God's most potent diseases, and on the borders of Nurgle's Garden the Swamp of Ages was crystallised during the War of Slime and Fire. Yet it does not all go Tzeentch's way, and none of his minions dare mention the disaster at Lom'nagini near their patron.

THE CHILDREN OF CHANGE

The daemons of Tzeentch are made of insanity and mayhem, the antithesis of order and law. In battle they present a maddening foe, chortling maniacally as they blast apart their enemies with dazzling spells and mimicking their agony as multicoloured flames burn away their victims' souls.

Tzeentchian daemons are physical manifestations of raw arcane energy, warped to reflect different aspects of their patron. As befits the Changer of the Ways, the natures of his minions vary greatly, although each is blessed with a portion of their master's magic and cunning. So infused are they with magic that the air about them takes on an unearthly glimmer, while their own colours and even material stability shift, so that sometimes they appear corporeal, and other times bafflingly illusive. As daemons, they have need for neither nourishment nor rest, and they cannot be slain as can mortal creatures. It is possible to destroy a daemon's physical shell, but doing so only sends its spirit back to the Realm of Chaos where it begins the painful process of reforming. The length of time this takes depends upon the daemon's size, strength, and, most importantly, whether or not the being still carries their god's favour.

It is difficult in the extreme for any one daemon to hold Tzeentch's attention for long, for the god is not inclined to rouse from his introspections. So immersed is he in his weighty schemes that it has been many ages since Tzeentch's physical form left the Impossible Fortress at the heart of the Crystal Labyrinth, his kingdom in the Realm of Chaos. There, in the sanctum of the Hidden Library, the

Great Conspirator prefers instead to read the infinite skeins of fate and to send forth his daemonic legions to advance his ineffable plans.

The onrush of the daemon legions of Tzeentch is a sight that can send the sane into raving madness. The very air shimmers with polychromatic colours as an outpouring of pure sorcery bursts above the oncoming masses. Capering Pink Horrors chortle as they advance, summoning mystic bolts. Sullen Blue Horrors grumble behind, wreathed in azure fires, while bright yellow Brimstone Horrors dance around their feet. Like strange living mushrooms, Flamers bound by, mutagenic flames pouring from their twisted limbs. The skies meanwhile are filled with Burning Chariots and shoals of predatory

Screamers. Looming over all come the Lords of Change, avian nightmares that wield fell sorceries.

The lesser of Tzeentch's daemons, the Horrors, are created as slaves and given little autonomy. It is their lot to follow orders given by those of higher rank, although even to these Tzeentch has bequeathed an unquenchable capricious streak. Other daemons, however, are granted far more self-reliance. The Heralds are Tzeentch's lieutenants – blessed with cunning minds and devious ambition, they lead the hordes in battle. The greater daemons known as Lords of Change are the most powerful of Tzeentch's immortal minions. These towering avian creatures are gifted near-total freedom to pursue Tzeentch's goals. It is they who set champions, Heralds and cults upon their courses, and it is they who most often direct the legions in a complex and ever-changing plan.

After Tzeentch issues commands to his armies, he contemplates their infinite effects, gazing upon his creations with fascination, eager to watch his children plot, deceive and manipulate even their own forces in order to further their ambitions. He avidly watches the unravelling of every strand of fate, each a small part of his Great Plan – though in the end, all fates are woven into one, and its outcome is doom.

THE SCINTILLATING HOSTS

To mortal eyes the kaleidoscopic daemon hosts of Tzeentch are impossible to distinguish from one another. There is method to the madness, however, although none save perhaps the Architect of Fate himself can truly follow all the ever-changing configurations.

Tzeentch's forces are subtly varied, their compositions often in flux. This fluid organisation pleases their patron, and is quite the opposite of Khorne's militant and hierarchal cohorts or the cyclical formations that serve Nurgle. Each convocation is led by a mighty Lord of Change, and is divided into nine hosts, each of which is led in turn by a subordinate greater daemon, Herald, or other powerful minion. The convocation's master may occasionally commandeer one of its hosts himself, should such a course of action appear propitious. All of Tzeentch's daemons are dedicated to furthering their patron's rule, but go about their tasks favouring particular methods depending on the convocation to which they belong. For instance, the daemons of the Grand Cabal worship Tzeentch in his role as Great Conspirator, and prefer espionage, intrigue, politics and clandestine sorcery to achieve their aims. The Transcendental Change, meanwhile, rely heavily upon the power of mutation, using transformational magics to wreak immediate and traumatic physical alteration. Although any of Tzeentch's daemons can appear in all of the different convocations, some show a proclivity for specific types. For instance, Flamers always feature prominently in the Eternal Conflagration, while the complete anarchy of the Unbound Flux typically centres around cavorting masses of Horrors.

Each of the convocations strives to garner the lion's share of their master's praise. As one would expect from the minions of Tzeentch, there is no end to their machinations as they push their own agendas while sabotaging those of their rivals. When the Great Schemer weighs the tributes paid to him and proclaims his judgement, the sigils of each convocation writhe upon the Shifting Pyramid of Yrch deep in the Crystal Labyrinth, blazing into new hierarchical order. The nine most favoured are each granted control of one of the Fractal Fortresses, and their fallen are resurrected more quickly from the Nine Gates. Not surprisingly, this new order can turn quickly – as fickle as Tzeentch himself.

The Lord of Change craned its long neck, looking down upon its summoner with bemusement and something else in its ancient, flickering eyes. 'Tzanarrr…' the voice of the daemon was low and purring. 'Why have you called upon me?'

For a moment the Magister attempted to meet the gaze of the greater daemon, but soon bowed his head. 'My Lord, I beseech a boon. Our enclave has been discovered. Even now Sigmar's champions are coming.'

The iridescent plumage of the Lord of Change shimmered as its gaze shifted towards the sacrificial victims strewn about the chamber's floor. 'Tell me Tzanar, this binding ritual – have you done it correctly?'

The Magister was accustomed to daemons and their deflections, and refused to be sidetracked. 'Bring forth your armies,' he begged. The sounds of battle could now be heard outside the hidden sanctuary. The Lord of Change laughed, at once like breaking glass and the distant call of crows.

'Three times three the offerings be,' said the daemon as it strode beyond the circle of blood-scrawled glyphs. 'One of the souls you offered was already mine, Tzanar.' Horrified, the Magister looked at the sacrifices to see only eight bodies and the fading illusion of the phantom ninth. 'Nonetheless, I am still inclined to help your cult. However, a few of the plan's details will have to change. I will require a few concessions…'

THE FLESH ASCENDED

Not all who are daemons begin their existence as such. El'an'zeth, the Ninefold Promise, was once a mortal servant of the Great Schemer, granted the gift of daemonhood after a lifetime spent gathering forbidden knowledge and lost secrets. He now stands eternal guard over the library-city of Uzalith.

Those who worship Tzeentch do so for power, knowledge and immortality. Many find their way into Arcanite Cults, wherein secrets must be unlocked and trials passed to ascend through the hierarchy. So it was for El'an'zeth, the Ninefold Promise, whose mortal name was Elias. Naturally gifted in the arts of sorcery, keenly intellectual and mercilessly acquisitive, Elias joined a cell of the Guild of Summoners, hidden within the winding volcanic caverns of Vindicarum. Many victims he sacrificed and nine arcane prizes he seized as he climbed through the ranks. Elias avoided the pitfalls of pride and avarice that would have blasted the minds of lesser souls – he even navigated the warped corridors of a Silver Tower, returning with boons of esoteric wisdom and mutation that paved his way to daemonhood. So runs the path to glory for those with the strength and willpower to walk it, for much may be gifted to those who dedicate themselves wholly to the Changer of the Ways.

NINE SHALL BE THEIR NUMBER

Each of the convocations has its own symbol, but only nine such icons can occupy the prime positions upon the Shifting Pyramid of Yrch. Those currently favoured by Tzeentch have held their status since the beginning of the Age of Sigmar and beyond, but – as ever – change is inevitable…

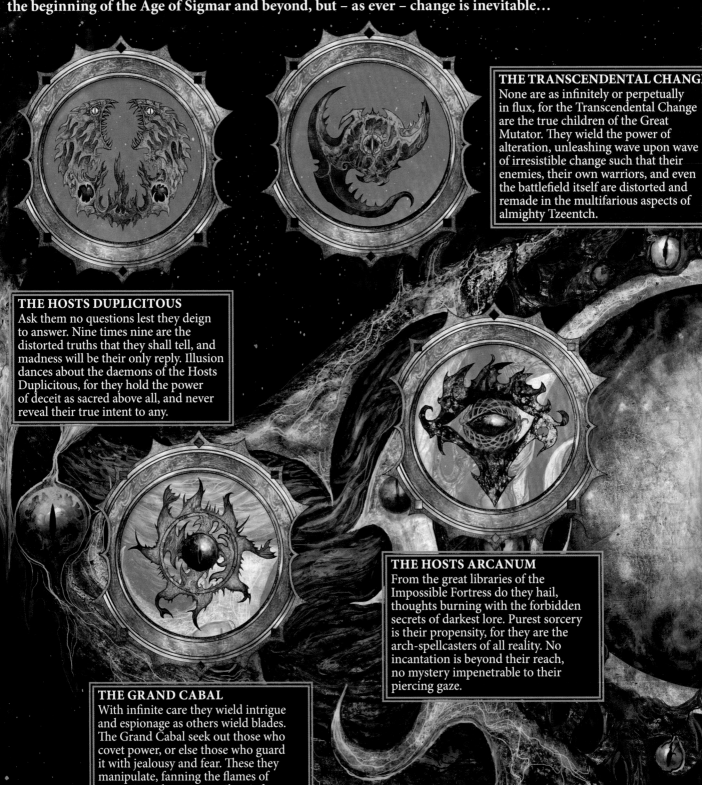

THE TRANSCENDENTAL CHANGE
None are as infinitely or perpetually in flux, for the Transcendental Change are the true children of the Great Mutator. They wield the power of alteration, unleashing wave upon wave of irresistible change such that their enemies, their own warriors, and even the battlefield itself are distorted and remade in the multifarious aspects of almighty Tzeentch.

THE HOSTS DUPLICITOUS
Ask them no questions lest they deign to answer. Nine times nine are the distorted truths that they shall tell, and madness will be their only reply. Illusion dances about the daemons of the Hosts Duplicitous, for they hold the power of deceit as sacred above all, and never reveal their true intent to any.

THE HOSTS ARCANUM
From the great libraries of the Impossible Fortress do they hail, thoughts burning with the forbidden secrets of darkest lore. Purest sorcery is their propensity, for they are the arch-spellcasters of all reality. No incantation is beyond their reach, no mystery impenetrable to their piercing gaze.

THE GRAND CABAL
With infinite care they wield intrigue and espionage as others wield blades. The Grand Cabal seek out those who covet power, or else those who guard it with jealousy and fear. These they manipulate, fanning the flames of paranoia and avarice until an inferno arises that none can survive.

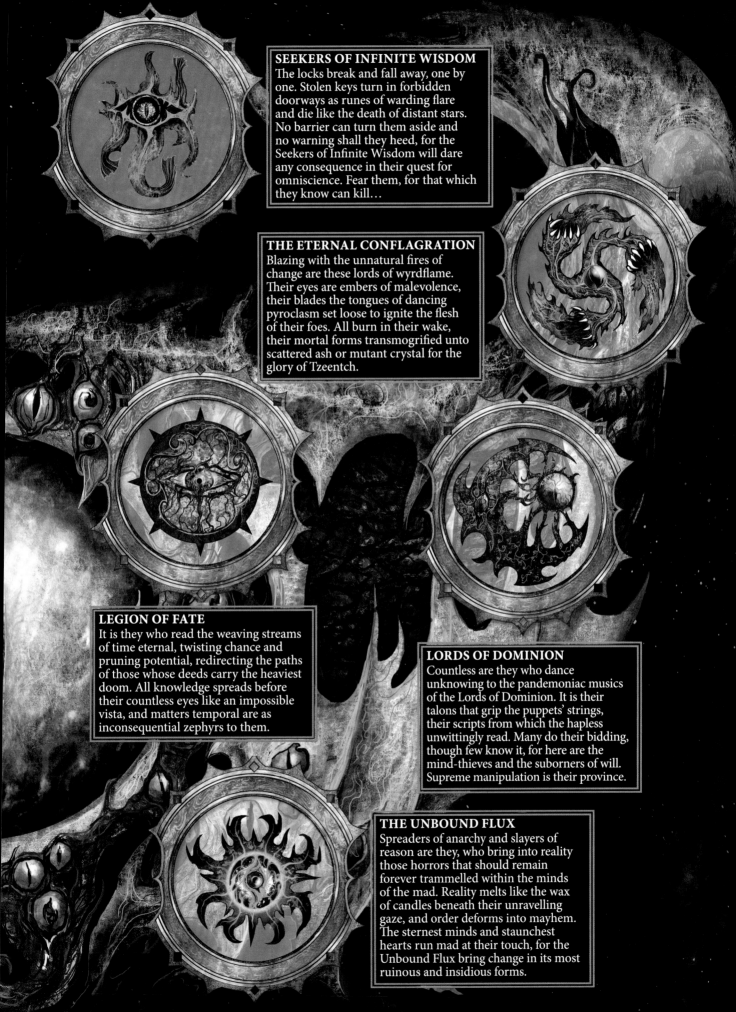

SEEKERS OF INFINITE WISDOM

The locks break and fall away, one by one. Stolen keys turn in forbidden doorways as runes of warding flare and die like the death of distant stars. No barrier can turn them aside and no warning shall they heed, for the Seekers of Infinite Wisdom will dare any consequence in their quest for omniscience. Fear them, for that which they know can kill…

THE ETERNAL CONFLAGRATION

Blazing with the unnatural fires of change are these lords of wyrdflame. Their eyes are embers of malevolence, their blades the tongues of dancing pyroclasm set loose to ignite the flesh of their foes. All burn in their wake, their mortal forms transmogrified unto scattered ash or mutant crystal for the glory of Tzeentch.

LEGION OF FATE

It is they who read the weaving streams of time eternal, twisting chance and pruning potential, redirecting the paths of those whose deeds carry the heaviest doom. All knowledge spreads before their countless eyes like an impossible vista, and matters temporal are as inconsequential zephyrs to them.

LORDS OF DOMINION

Countless are they who dance unknowing to the pandemoniac musics of the Lords of Dominion. It is their talons that grip the puppets' strings, their scripts from which the hapless unwittingly read. Many do their bidding, though few know it, for here are the mind-thieves and the suborners of will. Supreme manipulation is their province.

THE UNBOUND FLUX

Spreaders of anarchy and slayers of reason are they, who bring into reality those horrors that should remain forever trammelled within the minds of the mad. Reality melts like the wax of candles beneath their unravelling gaze, and order deforms into mayhem. The sternest minds and staunchest hearts run mad at their touch, for the Unbound Flux bring change in its most ruinous and insidious forms.

GIFTS OF TZEENTCH

Not all gifts from the Changer of the Ways come in the form of mutations or spells. In the Crystal Labyrinth, artefacts, weapons and armour are forged through eldritch means or ensorcelled by powerful Lords of Change.

1.   2.   3.   4.   5.

1. CHANGEBLADE
Those struck down by this ornate sword are transmuted in an instant to a horrific mass of tentacles and spines. Reborn as a Chaos Spawn, their new lives are as painful as they are short.

2. WAND OF WHIMSY
This peculiar stave was carved from the bones of Lord Krysothos, he who dared to steal a portion of Tzeentch's sorceries from the Nonesort Libraria. Though the greater daemon met a distressing end, his bones retain the ability to steal magic from those nearby and gift it to the wielder.

3. THE STAFF OF TOMORROW
This staff, borne by Kairos Fateweaver, is taller than a glimmerleaf tree and bound with countless enchantments, giving its wielder extensive knowledge of that which will soon come to pass.

4. PYROFYRE STAVE
Wreathed in warpflame, this staff glows white-hot at all times. A daemon with willpower strong enough to wield it finds the flames he conjures billowing into mutagenic infernos.

5. AMBITION'S END
When it cleaves the flesh of its victim, this strangely shaped weapon spills not only blood, but knowledge. One struck by it in anger is wounded grievously in mind as well as in body, becoming little more than a drooling simpleton as his lifeblood ebbs away.

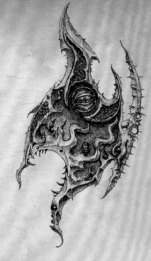

6. VHENTER'S VULCHARC
The Vulcharc is a carrion creature so twisted by the power of Chaos that it hungers for magic. Vhenter's Vulcharc has a penchant for the subtle spells of Ulgu.

7. THE SCROLLS OF SECRET IRE
It is said that upon these scrolls the hidden hatreds of those nearby are written in the form of riddles, giving the reader a chance to discern the secret agendas of both his allies and rivals.

8. SPITEFUL SHIELD
This shield possesses a baleful sentience. When an attacker has a killing thrust turned aside by the shield's strange protrusions, he will find he has sunk his weapon into his own flesh instead.

9. PARADOXICAL SHIELD
This shield exists as both a physical and spiritual artefact. It fills those nearby with glimpses of every death its wielder would have suffered had not the shield saved him. The shield is not fussy about who knows of its prowess — these involuntary visions have crippled many a foe in battle.

10. THE PORTALGLYPH
The mad mage Azjhat created the Portalglyph, intending to lure daemons to his service. Alas, he crafted his own demise. Though a crowd of fiends answered his summons, they bore him through his own gateway and into an eternity of terror.

11. BURNING CHARIOT DISC
Those Discs of Tzeentch that form part of an Exalted Flamer's chariot still have a strange awareness of their own, gazing with unblinking scrutiny at those who ride them into battle — perhaps to serve them all the better, or perhaps to pitch them to their deaths at a critical moment.

a	dh	gz	m	s	v
ar	e, ii	h	n	sh	w, uu
ak	f	i, ee	o	t, tz	y
bh	gh	kw, qu	ph	u	z, zh
ch	gu	l	rh	ui	

In addition to cryptic symbols and magical sigils, the servants of Tzeentch use a variant of the Dark Tongue.

TZEENTCH ARCANITES

Tzeentch does not rely on his daemon armies alone to conquer the Eight Realms. The Changer of the Ways has lured many mortal followers to his inscrutable cause. The Arcanites and their growing cults play a crucial role in the Great Schemer's plots of conquest.

Like his brothers, Tzeentch has corrupted countless mortal servants. Once, they belonged to tribes of men, but they became ensnared, lured by promises of power, glory, forbidden lore and immortality. Great champions rose, gathering those that followed the dark paths into armies, and during the Age of Chaos their conquests spread across the Mortal Realms, furthering Tzeentch's ineffable plans. Yet those slaves to darkness were not enough to satisfy the Changer of the Ways. In his infinite cunning, Tzeentch created other types of mortal armies, although they were far less conspicuous.

Whether veiled by illusionary magics or hidden as part of a clandestine society, the Arcanites have grown in power and number. Although some of these armies – or cults as they call themselves – have existed for generations, only recently have they begun to make their nefarious presence felt in the Mortal Realms. Some made their lairs in secret forest clearings or places rich in eldritch energies; others were secreted right under the noses of the forces of Order. As Sigmar's new cities grew, so too did the Arcanites, spreading like some hidden malignancy.

Although typically covert in nature, when the time is right the Arcanites strike, unleashing a bombardment of sorcerous destruction. Kairic Acolytes, their faces obscured by cryptic masks, chant sizzling arcane bolts into existence. Any foes that survive must then face the Acolytes' blades, along with those of the Tzaangor warflocks.

The Tzaangors are avian beastmen who serve Tzeentch, their unnatural instincts and animal savagery augmented with a keen, if cruel, intelligence. The Tzaangor elites – the Enlightened and the Skyfires – ride the air atop scintillating Discs of Tzeentch. Towering over all, hulking Ogroid Thaumaturges hurl roiling fireblasts from which spring Horrors, before lowering their mighty horns to charge the foe. The leaders of the Acolytes are the most powerful of them all. Fatemasters are cunning warriors surrounded by an aura that alters destiny to their favour. Magisters are master sorcerers who blast the enemy into swirling motes of multicoloured light or transmute them to crystal; crackling shields of magical power spark and flare as enemy blades and bolts rebound harmlessly against their incantations. The Tzaangor Shamans, meanwhile, ride upon daemonic discs and cause the air to crackle with mutagenic spells, transforming foes into other Tzaangors. With shouted commands these twisted cabals direct their covens across the battlefield, anticipating events before they happen.

After battle Arcanite Cults disappear – fading back into the hinterlands while covering their tracks with illusions, or once again assuming false guises to live undetected amongst the unsuspecting populations of the growing cities of Order. In the wilds, fell flux-cairns are raised, while in settlements, feuds are ignited and illicit political alliances forged. Once returned to obscurity, the cults recommence their secret plots. Foul rituals summon daemons, dark rites pinpoint the locations of arcane artefacts and places of eldritch power, and events are manipulated to twist fate in Tzeentch's favour. Always, the Arcanite Cults grow – luring in further conspirators, beguiling the power-hungry or even corrupting newcomers, transforming them into outcasts or mutants. Insidiously, Chaos spreads, while each cult awaits their next task. It will not take long, for Tzeentch has many plans, and change is coming…

THE ARCH-CONSPIRATORS

Always at the dark heart of an Arcanite Cult there will be a sorcerer, the founder of the cult, the leader of the army and the interpreter of Tzeentch's divine will. Forming a cabal around themselves, the leader grows their cult – amassing a secret army to strike in the name of the Changer of the Ways.

A scribe pores over dusty books, seeking reward for his research, answers to his many questions. What would an individual sacrifice to possess arcane knowledge? How far would one debase oneself to unlock a secret hidden for untold ages? Thus are many of the brightest minds led astray, lured onwards in a quest for enlightenment. One secret leads to another until, by slow increments, a soul has bartered away far more than they ever meant to. There can be no turning back, for those touched with the faintest trace of Chaos would do anything to avoid the agents of Order hunting them down and dragging them into the open. It is

in this manner, preying upon those who are most zealous in their search for arcana, that the Arcanite Cults recruit.

Cults are built around one or more powerful sorcerers. Driven by Tzeentch's unknowable will, a Magister, Tzaangor Shaman or Fatemaster lays the foundations, taking on apprentices worthy of their magical teachings and seeking others that can be taught. So it was with Tri'chlan, who formed the Cult Esoteric, a secret order dedicated to plumbing the depths of the most forbidden eldritch arts. Tri'chlan had long ago sold his soul to Tzeentch in exchange for vast knowledge, thus becoming a Magister – a sorcerer granted many dark gifts. Concealing his fall to Chaos with powerful illusions, Tri'chlan maintained his position

R olvidi did not know the man who had interrupted his illuminating work, but recognised the contorted hand gesture. He discerned the nine code words in the man's idle chat, and quickly put down his quill and hurried through the archival stacks towards the rendezvous site. Something was wrong. The hallways were more crowded than usual at this time, and from beneath his hood Rolvidi peered out, anxious to mark any telltale signs that might alert him to the presence of any of his fellow Acolytes amongst the crowds. He saw none. Commotion and raised voices came from the Great Hall ahead, and Rolvidi arrived to witness a group of hulking Stormcast Eternals surrounding someone. He jostled through the gathering crowd until he could see that it was a scribe whom he had seen before but never spoken to. Rolvidi was unsure whether he was even an Acolyte.

'You bear the mark of the traitor,' boomed the leader of the armoured giants. 'Justice will be done!' Even as one of the Judicators grabbed the scribe by the arm, Rolvidi felt the hairs on his neck rise. A sizzling bolt of pure iridescence seared overhead, striking the Stormcast leader and holding him, writhing, for a moment, before felling him. All eyes watched as his armour bulged, split, and tentacles wriggled out of the cracks.

'The justice of tyrants is not justice,' shouted a voice from atop the stairwell. Tri'chlan, the Magister, was revealed in his true form. 'Brothers, sisters, it is time!' he called. At those words, the hall shimmered. Rolvidi did as he was bade – discarding his illusions, he donned his ritual mask and drew his blade. A hot rush of adrenaline surged up his spine as he saw that the crowds around him had done the same. Grinning, he charged.

within the learned halls of the Grand Academy – a temple of enlightenment in the city of Hammerhal Ghyra. There, he sought those who, like himself, were questing for hidden knowledge, frustrated by the foolish barriers put in place by the Collegiate Arcane and the Eldritch Council that forbade the study or use of Chaos energies. Most aspirants were rejected – they lacked the proper conviction, or their abilities were not advanced enough. Those who passed were annointed as Kairic Acolytes, and their true training began.

It is a rare cult that is led merely by a single sorcerer, for its commander typically forms a cabal – a small inner circle of leaders, all of whom are masters of sorcery. New cultists must be recruited and trained, with those that pass ritual testing forming into covens. All the cultists as well as any meeting sites must be hidden from detection.

Secrecy is at the heart of the cabal and a great portion of their magical powers are directed towards concealing their cult's growing numbers. In this way, many cults have been seeded across the Mortal Realms, with only Tzeentch knowing the exact number and location of them all.

'Much knowledge is within easy reach, one only needs the stomach to seize it. My new brethren have taught me as much. Now, pass me my blade – the book says nine intact tongues are required for the Gibberhex to work, and I fear I did spoil the last one.'

- Rynald Ozkor,
Kairic Adept of the Cult Esoteric

As cults become larger they risk exposing their covert nature, and so change becomes necessary. Upon filling their cabal and nine covens to their sacred numbers, a cult will split, its members branching out, as Tri'chlan's once did when it sowed the seeds of the mutation-worshipping Cult of Blessed Transition. Such is the way of ambition, and such is the way of Tzeentch. Indeed, it is the ambitious that first seek entry into one of these hidden societies, eager to learn its secrets, to rise from Acolyte to Adept, to join the inner cabal, and finally to lead a cult themselves. Each new stage of a cultist's advancement unlocks for them further lore, which they voraciously absorb. All coven members compete for their leaders' praise, while the cabal seeks dark blessings from even higher powers, calling upon either Lords of Change or upon almighty Tzeentch himself.

SECRETS OF THE CULTS

Arcanite Cults are secretive, clandestine operations hidden by illusion and deceit. Although they are dedicated to the cause of change and the downfall of Order, there is some method to the madness of the organisation that binds together each cult.

An Arcanite Cult is a major assemblage of mortal Tzeentch-worshippers, ranging from factions of barely a hundred souls to vast organisations numbering in the thousands. Each cult is led by a small but powerful group of warrior-sorcerers known as a cabal, and may have further allies in the form of henchmen and honoured guests.

Every one of the Arcanite Cults is utterly dedicated towards fulfilling the aims of their deity, but like the convocations of Tzeentch's daemons, each cult does so by favouring one of their god's many aspects. For instance, those that flock to the banners of the Cult of Oracles are steeped in precognitive omens, portents and prophecies – their actions, intrigues and wars are all based around the predictive nature of their future-sight. The Cult of the Transient Form, however, favours mutations and change-magics to achieve their ends, while the Cult of a Thousand Eyes prefers to work behind a veil of secrecy, utilising spells of manipulation and control. Naturally each of the great cults regard themselves as superior to their brethren, and strives to maintain ascendancy. Open warfare between the cults is rare but not unheard of, and betrayals are frequent indeed.

An Arcanite Cult is usually comprised of three to nine covens. Covens are distinct groups of devotees made up of three separate groups – known as sects – in their turn. When a cult numbers more than nine covens it will keep to the sacred number by splitting apart, just as the globular aetherfish of Tzeentch's realm splits in two once it has glutted itself on the gales of magic. The extraneous covens then take a new identity and name. These splinter cults will often share the same colourations of armour and take aspects of their iconography from their parent cult, and will fight alongside them with only a faint whiff of treachery in the air.

HENCHMEN & HONOURED GUESTS

Many important cult rituals are carried out not by the cabal, but by its lieutenants and subordinates. Some of the ranks held by such individuals are exclusive to certain cults, but others are repeated across the spectrum. Perhaps the most commonly seen rank is that of Curseling, also known as an Eye of Tzeentch. This is a wizard whose body is host to a Tretchlet – a lesser daemon that grafts homunculus-like onto its bearer, conferring strange gifts and whispered counsel. Their ability to detect lies and glean a person's innermost secrets make Curselings excellent in their role of testing aspirants to the cult. The souls of those deemed unworthy are fed to the ravenous Tretchlet, thus forming a symbiosis between sorcerer and spirit. Stranger still are Ogroid Thaumaturges, hulking beings that blaze from within with supernatural flame. Little is known of these mysterious brutes, but they are steeped in dark lore and their command of the flames of Tzeentch is second to none. Within Arcanite Cults the Ogroid Thaumaturges bear titles like Thaumapriest or Master of Blueflame, for they lead the rituals that call upon warpfire, and teach its secrets to the Kairic Acolytes. Other types of lieutenant are less frequent, such as the Totemshriekers and Prophet-horns. It is not unusual for Arcanite Cults to summon daemonic aid – although in the end who controls whom is not always clear.

Occasionally, one of the Gaunt Summoners may assume command over an Arcanite Cult, or perhaps merely join it for a time to serve his own nefarious purposes, those of Archaon the Everchosen or the Great Architect himself. There are but nine of these terrifyingly powerful beings in existence, however, meaning their presence is greatly revered amongst cultists.

ARCANITE CULT STRUCTURE

As an organisation dedicated to the Change God, an Arcanite Cult fluctuates in size and composition as its members break away to form splinter groups or join other factions. Such fluidity conceals the true nature of the cult, and ensures that the influence of Tzeentch's followers is spread far and wide.

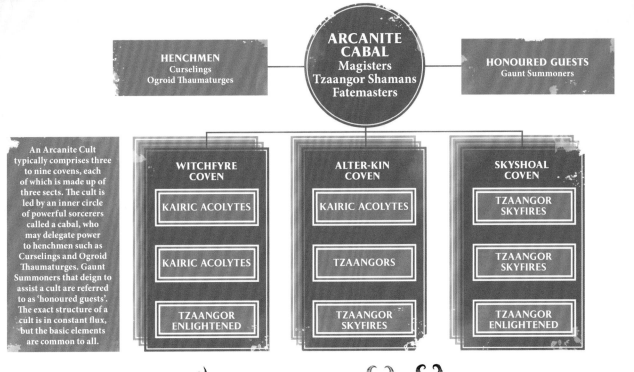

HENCHMEN
Curselings
Ogroid Thaumaturges

ARCANITE CABAL
Magisters
Tzaangor Shamans
Fatemasters

HONOURED GUESTS
Gaunt Summoners

An Arcanite Cult typically comprises three to nine covens, each of which is made up of three sects. The cult is led by an inner circle of powerful sorcerers called a cabal, who may delegate power to henchmen such as Curselings and Ogroid Thaumaturges. Gaunt Summoners that deign to assist a cult are referred to as 'honoured guests'. The exact structure of a cult is in constant flux, but the basic elements are common to all.

WITCHFYRE COVEN
KAIRIC ACOLYTES
KAIRIC ACOLYTES
TZAANGOR ENLIGHTENED

ALTER-KIN COVEN
KAIRIC ACOLYTES
TZAANGORS
TZAANGOR SKYFIRES

SKYSHOAL COVEN
TZAANGOR SKYFIRES
TZAANGOR SKYFIRES
TZAANGOR ENLIGHTENED

Alter-kin Covens are masters of mutating magic. To stand within the aura of change that surrounds them is to risk an agonising transformation.

Magisters, Tzaangor Shamans and Fatemasters may form the cult's cabal, though overall authority usually falls to one of these powerful individuals.

The Gaunt Summoners that align themselves to the Arcanite Cults are referred to as 'honoured guests', and are held in both fear and awe by the initiated.

Tzaangors that form covens with Enlightened and Skyfires fight with heightened ferocity, eager to prove themselves before their elevated kin.

The ruling cabal may employ independent henchmen, such as Ogroid Thaumaturges or Curselings, if it will further their arcane goals.

Witchfyre Covens are formed of Kairic Acolytes who demonstrate an aptitude for conjuring the fires of change, along with their Tzaangor Enlightened escort.

THE MARKS OF CHANGE

In times of war, arcane symbols previously concealed by a cult's members beneath voluminous robes or by subtle glamours are brazenly borne upon armour, banners and shields. The icons of branching cults usually preserve the colours or certain aspects of their progenitor cult's symbol.

Wisps of flame circling an all-seeing eye is the sigil of the wyrdfire-obsessed Pyrofane Cult.

Strange flowing forms representing continual evolution mark the icon of the Cult of the Transient Form.

Some say that the inner circle of the Cult Cognita know the truth behind Slaanesh's long absence.

The scrying orb is the sigil of the Cult of Oracles, who seek to disrupt the natural order of the stars.

It is the aim of the Guild of Summoners to bind no fewer than nine Lords of Change to their cult's service.

The Eldritch Cult whisper in the ears of a great many frustrated and ambitious novices of the Collegiate Arcane.

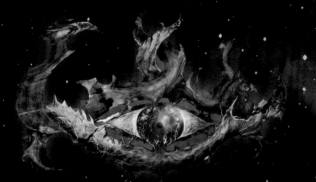

The Eye Entwined is the sign of the Cult of Twisted Fate, who revel in cruel ironies on a grand scale.

A multi-eyed crescent is used by the Cult of a Thousand Eyes. Their many spies and agents are scattered across the realms.

The icon of the Cult Pandemonious terminates in a ravening, soul-hungry maw, the change that consumes.

REVEALED IN THEIR TRUE FORMS

When, at last, the Arcanites shuck away illusionary disguise and emerge for battle, they do so proudly displaying the colours and icons of their cult. Indeed, once they are revealed, these markings transcend their status as symbols of forbidden association, becoming the regalia of open war.

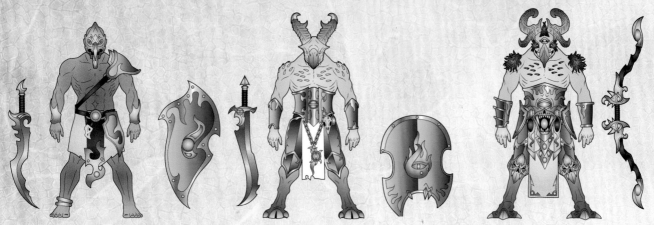

The Kairic Acolyte, Tzaangor and Tzaangor Skyfire above bear the colours of the Cult of the Transient Form. All warriors within a cult usually bear the same colours, but the exact configuration of these hues may vary between its covens.

A Kairic Acolyte of the Twisted Fate.

The Distorter Cult bear blood-scrawl markings.

Anarchy is the goal of the Cult Pandemonius.

A golden warrior of the Guild of Summoners.

The Pyrofane Cult use flame-motif tattoos.

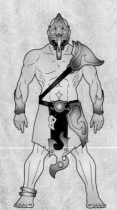

The Cult Esoteric follow the Magister Tri'chlan.

An Acolyte of the Cult of Blessed Transition.

White flames mark the Ninth Brotherhood.

The Burning Eye are a Pyrofane splinter cult.

The Blazing Hand abhor Nurgle's followers.

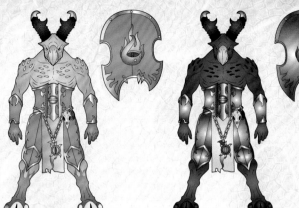

A pale-skinned Tzaangor of the Twisted Fate.

Crimson quills mark Cult Pandemonious Tzaangors.

Pink skin is the hallmark of Pyrofane Cult Tzaangors, while those of the Transcendental Flame are an icy blue.

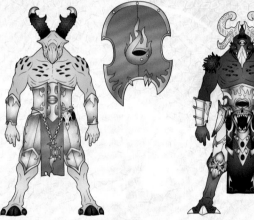

The Enlightened on the left hails from the Contortiad, while the blue Tzaangor belongs to its progenitor Distorter Cult.

A Tzaangor of the Guild of Summoners alongside an Enlightened from one of its splinter cults, the Lazulites.

A Vulcharc's plumage often becomes more vibrant and bewildering as it feasts on sorcerous energies.

As true creatures of Tzeentch, Tzaangor skin often manifests lurid colours and patterns. The variations are endless.

CHRONICLES OF DECEIT

As civilisation flourished once more in the Age of Sigmar, even mortals noticed the growing number of attacks by Tzeentch's minions. To observers the acts of aggression seemed random, yet the schemes of the Great Manipulator look purposeless only to those who cannot perceive their full complexity...

CORRUPTION IN EXCELSIS

The Cults of Twisted Fate and the Fated Path were uncovered in the city of Excelsis, leading to bloody battles through its streets. Seven more cults remain undetected...

UNDERMINING THE FOUNDATION

Sigmar and his growing pantheon fostered a new era of hope. Across the Mortal Realms cities were built and civilisations arose. Yet all was not as it seemed. Led by the Changeling, many of the new cities were founded upon realmstone – great deposits of solidified magic. Such lodes made corruption easier, and so were hundreds of new Arcanite Cults begun.

NEW RULERS IN THE GNARLWOOD

In Ghur, a coalition of Arcanite Cults fought a series of battles against the Bonesplitter tribes and Grot Scuttlings that dominated the Gnarlwood. After their victory, the Tzaangors of the Arcanites raised the largest flux-cairn yet, openly claiming the land.

THE FALL OF THE KINGDOM OF BUL'GHOH

In the Kingdom of Bul'ghoh in Ghyran, power struggles set Nurgle forces into a long civil war that culminated in their betrayal by the Clans Pestilens at the Battle of Bile. With perfect timing, the mastermind behind the infighting unleashed his own forces – Kairos Fateweaver sent forth nine daemonic convocations. The last stronghold of the Bulthrone might still have held out had several Arcanite Cults inside the citadel not thrown off their illusions and attacked.

TERROR AMONGST THE CLOUDS

Both golden and multihued clouds were seen across the Mortal Realms, but nowhere more so than in the high places of Chamon, the Realm of Metal. Aerial patrols from the Cities of Sigmar were sent to investigate, but none returned.

BATTLES OF THE BLURRED STARS

A series of nine spells of incredible might caused the stars to dance erratically. Thus did the sorcery of Tzeentch confound the slann. Seeking to restore their powers of premonition, the cold-blooded mages summoned many constellations of seraphon and sought out the loci of the fell magics. Nine great battles were fought, with great victories and losses on both sides.

BATTLE OF THE HEXWOOD

Stormcast patrols near Hammerhal Ghyra uncovered a hidden Tzaangor enclave, provoking its Shamans to summon a host of Flamers for aid. The warp-inferno unleashed caused the surrounding trees to uproot and lurch towards the Stormcasts, their branches transformed to squirming masses of tentacles.

WAR FOR THE DRYDEN FALLS

The invasion of the Kingdom of Bul'ghoh was not merely Tzeentch enacting revenge upon his brother, but the beginning of a larger plan. Kairos Fateweaver assembled daemon convocations and Arcanite Cults to cast a mighty spell. Alarielle and her Wargroves attempted to intervene, but were too late. So it was that massed change-magic crystallised the Dryden Falls.

THE RITES OF EQUILLAX

Over the Nine Days of Equillax prophetic dreams stirred Tzeentch's followers. Alter-kin Covens from splinter cults of the Transient Form turned entire human tribes to Tzaangors, daemonic hosts emerged to conduct rituals near loci of magical power and Silver Towers were seen across all the Mortal Realms.

WAR OF THE WYRDQUARTZ

No less than nine mountain ranges in Aqshy were riddled with strange crystal veins. Tzeentchian daemons sought to claim them, yet the Fyreslayers there brooked no invaders within mining territory claimed by their lodges.

CHANGING LANDSCAPES

AFTER AN EPIPHANY SIGMAR AROSE FROM HIS THRONE IN ALARM. UNDER THE LIGHT OF SIGENDIL, THE HIGH STAR, THE GOD-KING BEGAN TO PERCEIVE SOMETHING, A GROWING PATTERN. ACROSS THE MORTAL REALMS THE DAEMON LEGIONS OF TZEENTCH WERE SECRETLY TARGETING PLACES OF MAGICAL POWER. IN THE SHADOWS THE ARCANITE CULTS WERE RAISING FLUX-CAIRNS. TZEENTCH THE CUNNING WAS CONJURING A MIGHTY SPELL – SIGMAR COULD FEEL IT IN HIS BONES.

CRYSTAL FORTRESSES

Slave labour and stolen eldritch might was already transformed into hundreds of crystal fortresses across, and especially above, the Mortal Realms. More change was coming…

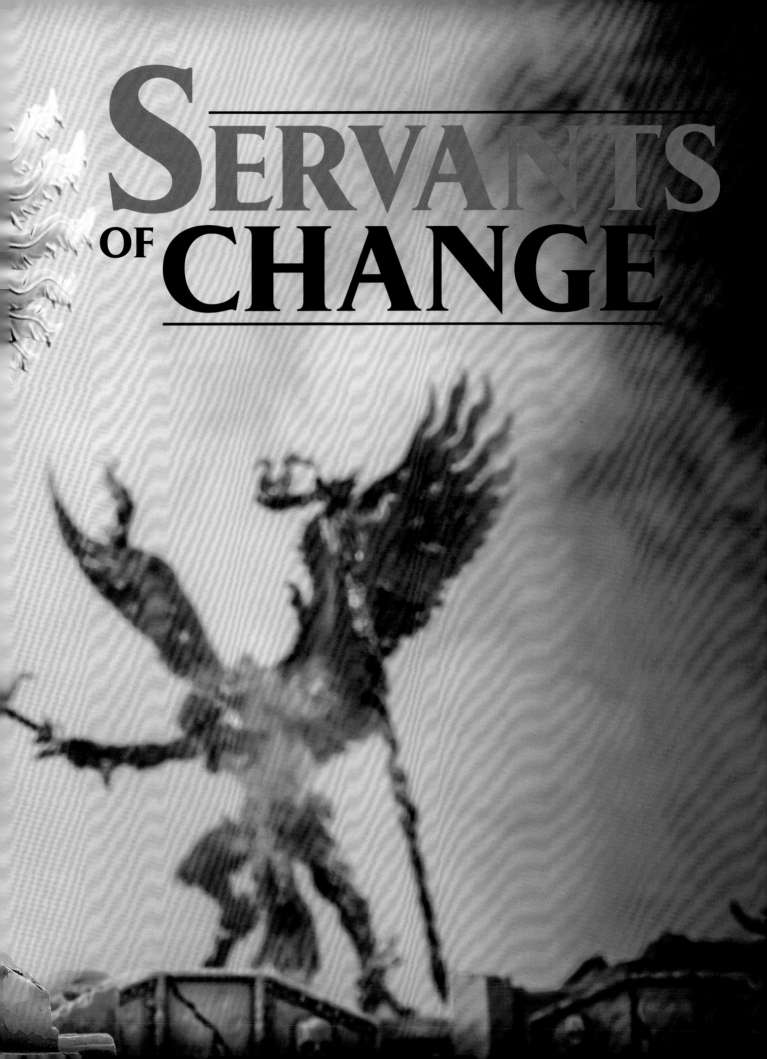

Servants of Change

LORDS OF CHANGE

The Winged Watchers, the Feather Lords. Lords of Change stride the battlefield in a prismatic aura of ever-changing magic, wielding their arcane powers to advance the myriad plots of Tzeentch. Their gaze pierces flesh to espy a mortal's hopes and dreams, laying bare all to the master manipulators.

Bursting with magical energies, a Lord of Change hurls pyrotechnic bolts of wyrdfire or splits reality with a gesture, sending enemies tumbling into the Realm of Chaos. As might be expected of greater daemons of Tzeentch, Lords of Change are mighty spellcasters. Indeed, it is pure eldritch energies that course through their bodies as blood pumps through that of a mortal. Rather more cunning and aloof than the greater daemons of the other Chaos Gods, Lords of Change will use their feathered pinions to carry them across the battlefield, ensuring that they fight the enemy on their terms and theirs alone. Although a Lord of Change typically uses magic and trickery to further its ends, it is still a

formidable fighter at need. With talons that can shred shields or pierce even sigmarite armour, countless heroes have underestimated these strange avian daemons with their wiry frames and brilliant wings, only to see their lances or swords shatter against their would-be quarry's immortal hide.

Of all of a Lord of Change's many terrible qualities, the most dangerous are its multilayered cunning and fathomless wisdom. Behind the inscrutable gaze of a Lord of Change lies a curious and callous mind, deeply intelligent, yet as uncaring of consequence as it is fascinated by it. The greater daemon's meddling in mortal affairs is not unlike a child playing

upon some gigantic anthill, poking at its inhabitants with a stick and laughing at the hopeless efforts of their defence. Nothing pleases these ancient beings more than to see a world broken then made anew, to redirect the course of a life or history itself, spilling hope upon the ground while raising the ambitions of others to such perilous heights that they are destined to fail.

As the purest manifestations of the Great Conspirator, the Lords of Change are unpredictable and shrewd. Perhaps their greatest weakness is that they are manipulative to the point of compulsiveness – continuing to twist plots long after their objectives are completed simply to see how far they

KAIROS FATEWEAVER

Even Tzeentch dares not enter the Well of Eternity, the vast receptacle of knowledge at the heart of the Impossible Fortress. It is the one puzzle the Great Sorcerer has not been able to solve, so in the name of understanding, Tzeentch hurled the Lord of Change known as Kairos into its endless pit. After being lost in the depths, Kairos eventually clawed his way back out. However, the journey changed him. Now, Kairos can perceive things that even Tzeentch cannot see. Kairos' right head sees possible futures as clear as day, while his left head sees the past without the petty colourations of perspective or bias. Yet this gift was not without toll, for both of Kairos' heads are now blind to the present; he cannot see time as it passes, only events that are yet to happen, or that have been.

For many ages of mortals Kairos Fateweaver sat at Tzeentch's right hand, stirring the Well of Eternity and whispering secrets of what will be, or truths about what has already come to pass. Whenever Tzeentch finally tires of unravelling eternity he sends Kairos on a mission – to lead an army, recover an artefact, or to follow some thread of fate through to its end. Although the Oracle of Tzeentch is vulnerable to physical attack – the future does not reveal itself swiftly enough to predict the to and fro of battle – Kairos has an unparalleled knowledge of magic. Tracing burning sigils in the air, the Fateweaver grants foes the gift of blessed mutation or hurls pyrotechnic blasts of warpfire, always keeping his eyes on the twisting threads of fate, awaiting the one moment when they should be manipulated to win the day.

can push their abilities. No few times have plans nursed for centuries been completed but the end goal foiled simply because the Lord of Change pulling the strings could not cease in its endless pluckings at the skeins of fate.

'Gates might bar your fortresses, but what guards your mind?'

- Yg'Rixirak, Eater of Ironies

The Lords of Change serve as the commanders of Tzeentch's armies. They are erudite tacticians, well versed in countless ploys and stratagems. Human champions, armies of the Slaves to Darkness, and Arcanite Cults move through the Mortal Realms at the command of Lords of Change, doing the creatures' bidding. If the daemons prefer to remain uncommitted in battle it is not through lack of ferocity, but merely because they like to oversee the movements of their forces and better control the flow of the fighting.

There are nine different ranks of Lords of Change – all with grandiose titles. The ranks themselves fluctuate in hierarchal standing, but the prefix of Exalted is applied to the title of the greater daemon that holds Tzeentch's highest favour at any one time. As the God of Change is fickle, however, even the most lauded daemons can fall out of favour in the blink of an eye. It goes without saying that Tzeentch's ranking criteria are indecipherable, and often appear completely arbitrary to even the most sagacious of his minions.

HERALDS OF TZEENTCH

The lieutenants of the daemonic convocations, the Heralds of Tzeentch help lead the multicoloured hosts to battle. Ambitious and daring, Heralds seek to enact swift and traumatic change – hurling the fires of Tzeentch at their foes before leading the charge, gibbering madly all the way.

Tzeentch created Heralds to lead his foot soldiers. These creatures are more powerful than Horrors, and are blessed with independent minds so that they might direct the capering masses. Unlike Horrors, Heralds do not morph into multiple beings when struck down. Instead, the magic of their creation has made them far stronger and more resilient than their smaller kin. Gifted sorcerers, Heralds can summon forth the fires of Tzeentch – wyrdfire of pink or blue – to blast enemies into bubbling pools of living sludge. Many Heralds also carry arcane tomes or scrolls from which they periodically recite incantations, augmenting their sorcerous might. Heralds are ambitious,

and eager to gain praise from the Lords of Change. Those that perform especially worthy deeds are gifted with Discs of Tzeentch or Burning Chariots, which greatly enhance their mobility, power and status.

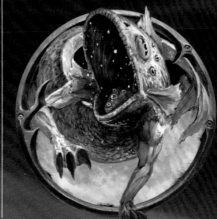

THE BLUE SCRIBES

Tzeentch created the Blue Horrors P'tarix and Xirat'p to record every spell in existence. They are like their kin in form and surliness, but are far more self-aware and powerful. The pair travel the realms on a Disc of Tzeentch seeking to transcribe every incantation they come across. Each is ever wary of the other's betrayal, for P'tarix can write magical symbols but cannot read, while Xirat'p can read his twin's writing, but cannot comprehend it. Squabbling between the two inevitably ensues. If threatened by enemies, Xirat'p reads at random from their accumulated scrolls while P'tarix stabs with his quill crafted from a Lord of Change's pinfeather.

THE CHANGELING

Amongst the greatest of Tzeentch's servants, the creature known as the Changeling personifies his patron's aspect as the meddlesome deceiver, the trickster supreme. Able to shape-shift into any form, none know the daemon's true identity, for it goes cowled and cloaked when not in disguise. Indeed, the Changeling has worn so many different guises throughout the long ages that even it cannot remember its original form.

The Changeling uses manipulation and deception to achieve that which martial strength alone could not. It assumes whatever face will allow it to further its machinations, seamlessly impersonating any other being it chooses no matter how big or small, mighty or meek. The Changeling has taken the forms of warriors and wizards, master thieves and trusted advisors. Its most recent coup was to impersonate Valius Maliti – the mastermind architect who helped build the foundations of all the Cities of Sigmar. During its time in disguise, the Changeling spread lies and misinformation, wove webs of falsehood, sought out others who might be ambitious enough to be corruptible, and planted seeds for future plots.

Sowing discord is what the Changeling does best, and its actions invariably lead to duels, battles and even prolonged wars. Although more an instigator than a fighter, once it abandons its false identity, the Changeling has no qualms about joining the fray personally. It can cast spells to blast the enemy with eldritch fire, and in combat its Trickster Staff adopts the qualities of its opponent's most powerful weapon.

FLAMERS AND SCREAMERS

In Tzeentch's legions the strange daemons known as Flamers serve as living artillery, blasting foes with gouts of flame before bounding forwards to finish them off. Screamers, meanwhile, glide through the air as a sea creature moves through water, swiftly striking anywhere on the foe's battle line.

FLAMERS

Flamers are bizarre creatures, even by the insane standards of the Realm of Chaos. Their tubular bodies randomly sprout gnashing maws and grimacing faces that mimic the last anguished cries of those they have slain. Flamers have no feet, but instead an inverted skirt of fungoid flesh which draws in air before expelling it by means of a powerful contraction. Thus, with loud whooshes of discoloured air, the Flamer can propel itself in leaps and bounds – ungainly perhaps, but capable of a fair turn of speed nonetheless. Flamers can clear obstacles with ease, and their strange mode of locomotion can even see them bounce across the surface of a body of water, their impacts sending up geysers of steam with each landing.

Although barely sentient, Flamers are extremely dangerous, for they revel in destruction. It is the flailing limbs of the Flamer that give the daemon its name. The long appendages end in tooth-lined stumps from which spouts fire. However, these are no normal flames, but the stuff of raw magic – multicoloured blasts that scorch the senses even as they char the body. Disturbing shapes and apparitions dance in those flames, and they have an unnatural habit of bursting back to life even long after they have been stamped out. The flames can be shot across long distances or spewed all around in the confusion of a melee. As the warpfires crackle and hiss, smaller flames spill to the ground and imitate the forms of those nearby. With glee and raucous laughter these eldritch simulacra mimic their enemies' death throes in a manner that is both mocking and disturbing. Soon, however, the diminutive images fade to nothingness. Their final shrieks of laughter can last for a considerable time after the flame-sprites disappear.

Exalted Flamers are champions of their kind and exude sorcery from every pore of their fungoid flesh. They are more capable of independent thought than their lesser kin, and often lead other Flamers or Horrors into battle. Some Exalted Flamers are carried into battle upon Burning Chariots, allowing them to rain billowing sheets of warpfire from on high.

SCREAMERS

Screamers are glimmering sky-sharks that ride upon currents of magic as a bird soars upon the breeze. Possessed of little more than hunting instincts, Screamers prey upon the shadow-souls of mortal creatures in the Realm of Chaos, along with anything blessed with magical powers. In the Mortal Realms, Screamers gather in undulating shoals and sweep across battlefields, especially targeting wizards. Festooned with fangs, horns and spurs they slash foes as they swoop past. When they find a suitable target, the Screamers dive, seeking to tear apart prey with their strange sucking maws lined with razor-sharp teeth. Large monsters must be particularly wary of shoals of Screamers, for they are capable of gouging out huge chunks of flesh with their lamprey-like mouths.

Being swift and agile, Screamers are highly sought after as riding beasts. Given their primal instincts, however, some transmuting magic must be used to break the daemon beast into a suitable steed. This new form, called a Disc of Tzeentch, maintains the Screamer's flat physiology but is otherwise transfigured during the binding ritual. The result is a great variety of Discs of Tzeentch – some are covered in eyes, while others are sheathed in living metal or covered in iridescent feathers.

BURNING CHARIOTS

Burning Chariots hurtle through the sky like strangely hued comets. Fiery discs of sorcerous metal shackled to a pair of Screamers, a Burning Chariot is typically commanded by an Exalted Flamer, although Heralds are known to also covet such arcane conveyances. Burning Chariots trail a wake of warpflame that can immolate those they fly over, and enable their riders to bring the gift of change to their enemies with joyous impunity.

HORRORS OF TZEENTCH

Capering, cackling daemons with a cruel sense of humour, the Horrors of Tzeentch embody the maddening inconstancy of the Change God. Even death does not quiet these flame-spewing monsters, as their bodies simply split apart to create smaller, but no less dangerous, fiends.

The Whirling Destroyers, the Bouncing Squealers, the Spinning Sourguts, the Cackling Flames – these are the Horrors of Tzeentch. Horrors are manifestations of pure Chaos, an unbound force that surges forwards, sometimes taking on a discernible form, at others blurring into a frantic mass of glowing colour as they scramble across the battlefield. Luminescent skin and high-pitched squeals of laughter identify Pink Horrors. They twirl frantically, flashes of energy

darting from their waving fingertips. In sufficient numbers, these Horrors generate enough magical energy to summon forth the wyrdfires of Tzeentch, which they hurl amidst much giggling to engulf the foe in sheets of magenta flame. When wounded, a Pink Horror exhales a last lunatic cackle before performing a final dramatic act – the swiftly decomposing ectoplasmic blob of the dying Pink Horror divides in two in a spasm of gyration, becoming two Blue Horrors.

Blue Horrors differ in temperament to their forebears. They are sullen and malicious, and wear perpetual scowls as they sneer and grumble their way through battle. Once spawned, the Blue Horrors fight alongside their fellows, adding a

deeper note to the incessant chortling glee of their pink brethren. Like their larger cousins, the Blue Horrors attempt to strangle foes with their large grasping hands. They too can conjure flames, but their conflagrations are blue in colour.

Should a Blue Horror be struck down it emits a drawn-out fatalistic groan before vanishing in a cloud of smoke. From those unnatural fumes prance living flames – a bright-yellow pair of Brimstone Horrors. These diminutive daemons have a spiteful and vindictive disposition – they eagerly claw and nip at the enemy with their tiny talons and fangs, while making every attempt to set them alight before they themselves finally gutter and burn out.

TZAANGOR SHAMANS

The Tzaangor Shamans are the most powerful of their kind, gifted by the Great Conspirator with arcane abilities, precognitive visions, and a savage intelligence. They begrudge all who are not Tzaangors, but a Shaman has the transmogrifying power to change all of that…

Those destined to become Tzaangor Shamans are born beneath dark omens – massed mutant births, strange stars, and powerful eddies of magical power. As a mark of their greatness, Tzaangor Shamans are gifted a Disc of Tzeentch, raising them literally as well as symbolically above their bestial kin. Tzaangor Shamans are held in highest reverence by their warflocks, for they see the Shaman as holding the greatest of boons – the ability to transmute other beings into Tzaangors. With a defiant hoofstomp and a crack of his staff, the Tzaangor Shaman unleashes his mutagenic spell. Those struck by the blue-tinged bolt fall to the ground writhing uncontrollably,

wracked with agonising contortions, before rising once more as glistening-skinned Tzaangors. This is not a Shaman's only power, for they also possess the gift of prophecy. Other Tzaangors say that when in a trance the Shamans spirit-walk into the Realm of Chaos to take commands from the Feather Lords. Upon emerging from such rituals, many Tzaangor Shamans migrate from their warflock, following a divine calling. Some leave to join a different Arcanite Cult, or to lead a coven upon some sacred mission. Those not called away continue to lead the warflocks, guiding them through many fell rites while directing the raising of flux-cairns, the magical

herdstones of the Tzaangors. It was Shamans that first showed the warflocks the wisdom of eating the tongues of their foes to gain their speech and insight. It is the Shamans who lead the hunt for Chaos creatures, subduing such monsters as Cockatrices or Mutalith Vortex Beasts, and marking their hides with the dark tongue, and it is they who know the secrets of distilling the blood of mages to boost the potency of their own spells. In battle the Tzaangor Shamans are no frail wizards. These bestial mystics swoop directly into the fray, slashing at the foe with ritual daggers and rending their flesh with wicked beaks and horns in the name of mighty Tzeentch.

TZANGHUR, GREAT CHANGER OF THE HEXHORNS

Born fully grown beneath a black moon, Tzanghur was marked for greatness from the beginning. It is he who leads the Hexhorns, an Alter-kin Coven of the Arcanite Cult known as the Inglorious Transition. They are change-bringers, a splinter cult of the Transient Form. Everywhere Tzanghur has led his coven – down the Valley of Skulls, through the Wyrmwood, and even within sight of the walls of the city of Excelsis – everywhere they have brought the gift of change. Beastmen, orruks and Bloodbound – all have had their miserable existences transformed in glorious service to the Changer of the Ways. Entire Tzaangor warflocks exist solely because of Tzanghur. As a reward from Tzeentch, the Shaman's cleft horn – caused by a parting shot from a fallen Stormcast Eternal – regrew in a single night. The lurid scar from an orruk blade over his right eye remains, however. Tzanghur does not question why he was only partially restored, for such is his god's inscrutable will.

OGROID THAUMATURGES

The cabals of all Arcanite Cults seek to recruit Ogroid Thaumaturges to their cause. Not only do the flame-wielding creatures bring with them magical secrets, but their muscle-bound frames and formidable horns make them truly fearsome adversaries in combat.

Shrouded in mystery and rumour, there is much speculation but little actually known about Ogroid Thaumaturges. There is no doubt, however, that the creatures are steeped in magic – their very skin writhes with arcane energies, as inner fires blaze eldritch sigils across their hulking bodies. In their rage, the telltale multicoloured flames of Tzeentch erupt about them, often centred around their totemic staves. Ogroid Thaumaturges are bestial in nature, possessed of enough strength to tear a man in two with their bare hands or drive their horns through even sigmarite plate armour. Although their might rivals that of a troggoth, the Ogroid Thaumaturges are not dumb brutes, but sorcerous beings possessed of cunning minds. It is said that they know more of the secrets of wyrdflame than any save the most accomplished spellcasters. They can summon coruscating blasts of the mutating fire from which Tzeentch's own daemons spring forth, a sure sign of the Change God's favour. Ogroid Thaumaturges are particularly revered in the Pyrofane Cult, where their flame powers are especially venerated by the Kairic Acolytes. Some Ogroid Thaumaturges lead a coven to battle, with Tzaangors especially flocking to the horned giants, while other Ogroids serve as bodyguards for the enigmatic Gaunt Summoners.

THE GAUNT SUMMONERS

The Gaunt Summoners stand high in the favour of Tzeentch, their spells able to twist landscapes and immolate armies in wyrdfire. When they deign to join Arcanite Cults they do so either to lead them on some nefarious cause at the behest of the Great Schemer, or to further their own ineffable aims.

Of the ranks of Tzeentchian Sorcerers there are few higher than the dreaded Gaunt Summoners. Each of their number could single-handedly shift the tide of a battle. Luckily for Sigmar and his allies, however, there are but nine such beings in existence, elevated to their lofty station by the Architect of Fate himself. Upon achieving that terrifying level of accomplishment, each Gaunt Summoner was gifted with even greater arcane power, a changestaff, a flying Disc of Tzeentch, and the key to one of the nine Silver Towers. These lairs of hidden knowledge are insanely complex machines, puzzle-fortresses beyond the scope of mortal minds. As a pastime, the Gaunt Summoners delight in letting

A Gaunt Summoner's Book of Profane Secrets perverts the ancient power of the Realmgates.

captives loose in their labyrinthine corridors, impossible dimensions and ever-shifting pathways, watching with amusement as they are slain in an infinite number of ways by the lethal creatures and devious traps therein. Those few that fight their way to freedom are granted boons, but such an occurrence is rare indeed.

When taking to the battlefield alongside an Arcanite Cult, the Gaunt Summoners are regarded with a level of awe normally reserved for Lords of Change. With but a word, these master sorcerers can call forth daemons from nearby Realmgates, or cripple the enemy by turning their own mental strength against them.

THE WILL OF THE EVERCHOSEN

Once, the Gaunt Summoners were given freedom by Tzeentch to pursue their own fates. In this the god was wise, as each of the mage-lords was obsessed with the accumulation of magical knowledge and power. In these pursuits, they brought Tzeentch great glory. Even the Gaunt Summoners' amusements – testing the mettle of warriors in their endless labyrinths – offered the Changer of the Ways occasional distraction. Yet Archaon – most powerful champion of Chaos – wished to possess the eldritch power of the Gaunt Summoners for his own.

Tzeentch himself watched on with great interest as Archaon sacrificed the lives of many of his followers seeking to discover the true names of the Gaunt Summoners, the only

way in which to bind their services. In this duel, Tzeentch was of two minds – the Gaunt Summoners belonged to him, yet on the other hand the attempts of each of the Dark Gods to persuade the Everchosen to serve them exclusively, rather than all of them equally, had failed. This both vexed and impressed Tzeentch, for it was not often that another could dictate the Great Conspirator's chosen course of action. In the end, Tzeentch reasoned that allowing Archaon to usurp dominion of the nine daemon-sorcerers would better serve the god's own ends, and so Archaon went on to win the names of all the Gaunt Summoners, never realising the subtle aid he benefited from along the way. Yet ever since, the Gaunt Summoners have chafed beneath the rule of Archaon and plot one day to rebel. Change is inevitable…

MAGISTERS

Wielding the power of raw magic to wreak change upon the battlefield, a Magister is a high-ranking sorcerer within an Arcanite Cult. They are secretive, cunning and so ambitious they will stop at nothing to lead their cult to victory and to advance still further on their path to glory.

Magisters are powerful Chaos Sorcerers that long ago sold their souls into the service of Tzeentch. Their badges of office include a Tzeentchian runestaff and a warpsteel sword, along with an array of mutations that are pleasing to the Architect of Fate, including third eyes, bristling quills and even jabbering heads embedded in their torsos. So favoured are they by their god that raw magical power flows through their veins, allowing them to draw upon the very essence of Chaos to infuse them with sorcerous might. When they harness such potent energies, arcane syllables spill from a Magister's lips in a continuous stream, and their hands trace eldritch symbols in the air with a speed that is almost impossible for the eye to follow. Those Magisters who drink too deeply from this font of magical energy are transformed into mindless Spawn, but a rare few are granted the ultimate reward – ascension to daemonhood and the status of Daemon Prince. Such is a goal that the Magister will ruthlessly manipulate others to achieve, including the members of his own cult.

A Magister's role varies depending on the cult to which they belong. Many are the undisputed leaders of their cult, whilst others share command with the other members of their cult's cabal. Almost regardless of their position, a Magister's title will be grandiose, such as Grand Vizier of Change, Exalted Potentate of Transformation or Keeper of Illusions. Many have secreted themselves within the Cities of Sigmar, either in some clandestine, hex-protected locale, or disguised by eldritch means to walk amongst the citizenry. As their patron is patient, so too are they, biding their time and nurturing their strength while sowing seeds of corruption. The time for open attack is coming, and each Magister longs to earn glory, and the resultant rewards, in the name of Tzeentch.

FATEMASTERS

Equipped with magical weapons and armour, a Fatemaster is not just a powerful warrior but a living conduit of destiny-twisting power. With a Fatemaster altering the strands of fate to turn the tide of battle in his cult's favour, few are the foes that the Arcanites cannot overcome.

A Fatemaster is a Chaos Lord dedicated to Tzeentch. Some Fatemasters command entire Arcanite Cults, others lead covens, while some perform more specialised roles such as enforcer, Keeper of the Realmgate, or Doomsayer. To attain the rank of Fatemaster, a warrior must not only prove their devotion to Tzeentch, but also show the cunning and quick thinking favoured by the Changer of the Ways. After all, the Arcanite Cults are Tzeentch's chosen. These are not foul-smelling and barbaric Slaves to Darkness armies, but erudite and clandestine warriors fighting a guerrilla war, often ensconced deep within enemy-held territory. More than simply bravery and martial skill are required

to pass the dreaded Nine Trials of Fate. It takes either an incredible amount of luck or intuition that surpasses anticipation. To duck the sweeping blade that moves faster than human reaction, to espy the treacherous ally before the betrayal – these must be done to not just succeed in the trials, but also survive them. Those few who complete the tasks are anointed

Fatemasters and sent to lead the secret enclaves of the Arcanite Cults. Before they do so, however, they are gifted mighty boons to better serve Tzeentch: a fireglaive, a soulbound shield, Chaos armour and a Disc of Tzeentch. In battle a Fatemaster streaks into the fray, leaving behind a wake of dismembered corpses – the gruesome aftermath of precision glaive-strikes and swooping dives from their bladed Disc. Hostile spells rebound off a Fatemaster's gleaming shield, but perhaps their most powerful gift is a fate-shifting aura – the ability to twist the very laws of causality in Tzeentch's favour, causing enemy arrows to hit armour rather than flesh, or guiding friendly blades to strike home instead of glancing astray.

Even as he reloaded his crossbow, Gunther's mind whirled. Here – how could the traitors be here, in their very midst? After dispatching the rest of the patrol, the cultist army had taken the square. The nearest formation had reformed and was heading straight for them, blades dripping with blood. At their fore was an armoured figure atop a strange floating disc that trailed blue flames.

'Take aim,' came the order from Sergeant Trass. 'Steady men… steady,' growled the old officer, as if he felt Gunther's quavering nerves. The cultists' outlandish masks glinted in the sunlight, and although he did not understand the words they were chanting, the sound made Gunther grit his teeth while sweat ran down his

back. At last the order came and the click-thwack sound of bolts being loosed rippled down the line.

'Reload,' Trass bellowed. As he fumbled for another bolt, Gunther could not help but glance upwards to see how many shots struck home. The advancing cultists were still in line, and closing the distance fast. Gunther's bolt clattered onto the cobblestones and he reached for another, missing the ensuing volley. Mouth agape, Gunther just stared. They were Freeguild Crossbowmen, paid and well trained. They simply could not all have missed. Not at this range. His eyes drew irresistibly to the armoured figure; Gunther watched the final volley, watched sparks of blue flash harmlessly. And then it was too late, and the slaughter continued.

CURSELINGS

Twisted of form and gifted with a cackling homunculus, Curselings are favoured lieutenants in many Arcanite Cults. Guided by the misshapen being melded to them, Curselings use their many dark blessings to further their ceaseless quest for arcane knowledge.

Few of Tzeentch's gifts can be understood, for the Dark God's true will is beyond the ken of mortal-kind. So it is with Curselings, those beings sometimes known as the Eyes of Tzeentch. Once they were rising sorcerers, acolytes of the dark arts that sought to further their arcane studies. Something, however, went wrong, as the secrets they had garnered coalesced inside their bodies to form an eldritch tumour of forbidden knowledge that grew until it was possessed by a malign sentience – a spirit-creature from the Realm of Chaos known as a Tretchlet. Like some monstrous parasite, it grows from the body of its host and gives constant hissing advice to seek further knowledge. The Tretchlet's Curse is thought to be brought upon those that learn a secret too many, or perhaps just the wrong one.

Although shunned by right-minded folk, Curselings are highly coveted by Arcanite Cults. Acting as lieutenants for the cults' cabals, Curselings sometimes fulfil the role of inquisitor, for Tretchlets have the ability to detect lies. Sucking air through their chattering teeth, the grotesque beings can smell out secrets and their questions can draw out hidden knowledge, traits invaluable to cults seeking arcane enlightenment. A trial by Curseling is also an effective way of determining whether new Acolytes are worthy of joining a cult.

Though they excel in the role of lie-seeker, in truth all Curselings hunger for battle. There, they are formidable warriors, but are most valued for their ability to glean an enemy wizard's spells and to hurl them back upon the caster. Nothing gives a Tretchlet more gratification or makes them cackle more maniacally than when they slay a wizard with their own spell.

TZAANGORS

Tzaangors are savage, avian-like beast-kin dedicated to Tzeentch. As such, they have been warped into shapes more pleasing to the Architect of Fate. Foes that underestimate the bestial cunning and fierce strength of the Tzaangors quickly fall before their sharp blades and gouging horns.

Strange trilling calls come from seemingly deserted woodlands, and flying shapes flit through sudden mists. Peering out from illusion-concealed lairs, the Tzaangors watch and wait. Although rarely seen, they have been massing their numbers, establishing strongholds and launching covert strikes. Soon, however, they know that the time will be ripe, and then they will rise to unleash their full fury.

Tzaangor origins are as multifarious as the plans of Tzeentch themselves. Some are Gor-kin corrupted – or elevated, as they might say – by a Tzaangor Shaman; others might be humans who have undergone horrific rituals. Others still are beast-children, mutants born of human parents and left to die, but instead found and raised by Arcanite Cults. Regardless of source, all recognise that they have been blessed by Tzeentch. Tzaangors are far more intelligent than other beastmen, and they look down upon their beast-kin, seeing themselves as evolved and their cousins as little more than brute animals. The strangely mutated minds of Tzaangors have become particularly attuned to magic and they are drawn to the arcane, seeking to hoard it. Tzaangors are also closely bound to the strands of fate, their animal instincts able to detect omens the way beasts scent prey upon the winds. Yet Tzeentch did not transform his chosen beastmen to seek magic alone – he also created them to kill. Many rituals prepare Tzaangors for war, culminating in the weapon-taking Tzaanwar, an unholy rite where the rent armour and broken weapons of foes are transformed into the resplendent gear worthy of fighters of Tzeentch. In battle the Tzaangor warflocks are led by a Twistbray champion, and they fight with savage skill, stabbing and hacking with curved swords or axes, as well as rending with horn and beak. As magical creatures they

draw energy from the proximity of Tzeentchian sorcery and others of their kind – the more groupings there are of nine Tzaangors, the more savage they become. Favoured Tzaangors are sometimes honoured with bearing their god's icon to war. These ornate totems can absorb the magical energies of nearby spellcasters, and are used by the Tzaangors to steal the arcane force which they use to grow their flux-cairns. Recently tapped eldritch powers can even be directed as bolts towards nearby foes.

Tzaangors whose deeds have caught the eye of their patron are rewarded with divine blessings. They are divided into two distinct groups, the Enlightened and the Skyfires, and are regarded by other Tzaangors as paragons of their bestial kind. Enlightened carry spears wrought of change-metal, and possess the strange ability to perceive echoes of past events around them. In combat many foes are driven mad as their darkest secrets are squawked out by the chattering Enlightened. Some Enlightened march to war amongst their lesser kin, inspiring them to greater acts of savagery, while others ride scintillating Discs of Tzeentch. Skyfires, however, exclusively ride upon Discs. It is their gift to see potential futures, but they can never speak of them. Skyfires are utterly silent bar the twang of their bowstrings as they loose their Arrows of Fate. Both groups are led by Aviarchs, the strongest and most cunning of their number.

Tzaangors can be found in every one of the Mortal Realms, where they live in the wild places, choosing locales rich in magic to raise their strongholds. In Ghyran this means near waterfalls or wellsprings, while in Aqshy this might be alongside volcanoes or fiery chasms.

There, Tzaangor Shamans tap into the magic to raise flux-cairns, which become repositories of stolen arcane might. Flux-cairns are surrounded by lesser herdstones – glyph-inscribed monoliths shaped in symbols sacred to Tzeentch. The longer a flux-cairn remains in place, the more the lands about it change. It is the Tzaangors' goal to use them to warp entire kingdoms, and eventually the realms themselves.

While Kairic Acolytes seek to build libraries of forbidden knowledge, the Tzaangors do the same but eschew books, for their Shamans copy dark learnings upon beast-hide, some of which is still attached to living creatures. Many Chaos beasts such as Ghorgons, Razorgors, Jabberslythes, Chimeras, Cockatrices, or Mutalith Vortex Beasts can be found alongside Tzaangor warflocks, all with dark script painted on, or carved into, their flanks.

KAIRIC ACOLYTES

They who speak the killing words, the Chanters of Change, the Altered. The Kairic Acolytes are the human cultists of Tzeentch, cunning infiltrators who have made dire sacrifices in exchange for knowledge or power. They walk amongst the unsuspecting, until the time for them to strike is ripe.

The robed cultists chant, not in a tribal rhythm that stirs the blood, but in an arcane tongue that chills it. From disturbing to painful, the tone fluctuates; the cadence halts, begins, and grates until each Acolyte summons a radiant ball of scintillating light. For an instant the spheres hang mid-air before streaking off towards their target in a roaring volley of sorcerous bolts.

Those who become Kairic Acolytes come from all walks of life – tribesmen led astray by an arcane calling, seekers of forbidden knowledge, and city-dwelling civil servants overeager to gain power. All share a driving ambition that marks them from the common man. It

is not by chance that such individuals cross paths with an undercover Acolyte, for the Arcanite Cults recruit aspirants, taking years or even decades to ensnare potential suppliants. The teachings of Tzeentch's worshippers preach that, given time, those who listen to their mind's night-time whisperings will one day serve the Architect of Fate.

In the end, only those that wholly commit are accepted into the cult. Many undesirables are weeded out and only the worthy can attempt the Kairic Test of Nine. Each cult has its own variations on these rites, but all end with the walk through warpfire. Those that emerge unharmed become

a Kairic Acolyte. Chanting arcane phrases that hurt the ears of the uninitiated, a scrawny scribe or frail council elder transforms. Flesh ripples and from nothing appear a curseblade and shearbeak helm, gleaming greaves and an Arcanite shield. Thus can a cultist, with mere words, transform themselves from ailing scholar or lanky apprentice to a muscle-bound ideal of the human form, and then back again. In this way, the Kairic Acolytes can infiltrate and subvert the very forces of those that hunt them.

Sects of Kairic Acolytes are secretive, with many continuously growing undetected in human tribes and cities

BROTHER GH'RHAN, ADEPT OF THE BLUE FLAME

By day Brother Gh'rhan is a scribe that toils in the Academia Veterum in the growing city of Phoenicium. In the evenings, however, his scholarly garb is eschewed in favour of the magical trappings of the Arcanite Cult of the Majestic Blue Flame. Brother Gh'rhan only feels truly alive when he speaks the magic words and his corpulent form melts away, replaced with the sleek, muscled body gifted him by his patron. Only behind his shearbeak mask does he feel like himself. Twice Gh'rhan has fought alongside his brethren, both times in operations outside the city. In the second battle, it had been he who led the remnants of his coven to finally fell the savage seraphon leader. That, and the failure of his former Adept, had earned Gh'rhan the promotion. He longs now to hear the coded word to attack the city itself. He longs to bring the revolution of change to those that have stolen the years of his youth with their futile and empty labours.

across the Mortal Realms. To maintain their secrecy, the more conspicuous aspects of their altered forms, and their meeting places, are concealed beneath illusions and sorcerous obfuscations. The Acolytes wear ritual masks and are careful to change out of sight of even their fellow cultists, so that none know the true identities of the other members. Great pains are taken to arrange meetings in hidden locations, where the Kairic Acolytes learn the secrets of magic from their leader – a Kairic Adept – as well as from any Magisters in the cult's cabal. In time, Acolytes all aspire to become powerful wizards, supremely confident that it will be they who master Chaos and never the other way around. Each level of advancement brings new secrets. To those Acolytes that show promise, boons are granted – arcane grimoires, talismans from the Crystal Labyrinth to boost arcane abilities or even a Vulcharc, a carrion bird so corrupted by Chaos so that it hunts and feasts upon magic.

Kairic Acolytes are tasked with manipulating events to turn destiny in their god's favour; an alchemist conducts disturbing research with dark magic, or a worker gang plots to burn down a nearby district, pinning the blame upon the different races that live amongst the Cities of Sigmar. Feuds are begun, political alliances torn asunder. Insidiously, Chaos spreads. Such is the way of Tzeentch, who does not favour frontal assault as does his brother god Khorne. Tzeentch's way is slower, chipping away at the foundation piece by piece until the entire structure collapses. When the cabal of an

Arcanite Cult feels the time is ready, they gather together, cast off their illusions, and strike. Chanting while they march, Kairic Acolytes pool their energies in order to barrage their foe with sorcerous bolts, drawing further arcane strength from any Tzeentchian spellcaster. In combat they close in a flurry of shimmering curseblades, chanting arrhythmically all the while.

ARMIES OF UNREASON

Daemons of Tzeentch led by Kairos Fateweaver fall upon the Hammers of Sigmar amidst a storm of wyrdflame.

Masters of sorcery and deception, the lords of Tzeentch's daemon armies are soul-blasting terrors on the battlefield.

Screamers glide above the battlefield on currents of magic, swooping down to eviscerate unsuspecting prey.

Horrors of Tzeentch split in two when they are slain, burying foes in a tangle of grasping hands and snapping maws.

Kairos Fateweaver

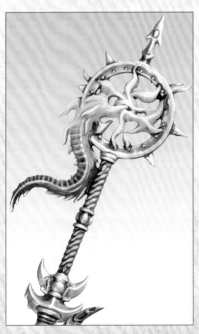

Lord of Change

Iridescent Horror

Pyrocaster

Pink Horrors

Flamers of Tzeentch

Brimstone Horrors

Blue Horrors

The Changeling

The Blue Scribes

Burning Chariot of Tzeentch

Herald of Tzeentch

Exalted Flamer of Tzeentch

Herald of Tzeentch on Burning Chariot

Shrieked war cries echo through mists of crackling magic as the Tzeentch Arcanites charge into battle.

The leaders of an Arcanite Cult are some of the most powerful spellcasters in all the Mortal Realms.

Twisted and degenerate, Tzaangors lope from the dark forests to slay their foes in the name of the Great Mutator.

Kairic Acolytes hurl sorcerous bolts before charging forth to slay the cult's enemies in a frenzy of slashing blades.

Tzaangor Shaman

Magister

Fatemaster

Ogroid Thaumaturge

Curseling, Eye of Tzeentch

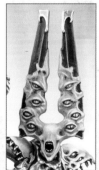

Gaunt Summoner

Tzaangor Enlightened

Aviarch

Tzaangor Enlightened

Tzaangor Skyfire

Aviarch

Tzaangor Skyfire

Tzaangor with Brayhorn

Tzaangor

Tzaangor Icon Bearer

Tzaangor Mutant

Tzaangor with Greatblade

**Kairic Acolyte with
Cursed Blades**

**Kairic Acolyte with
Cursed Glaive**

**Kairic Adept with Scroll of
Dark Arts**

**Kairic Adept with
Cursed Glaive**

**Kairic Adept
with Vulcharc**

ZYCLAW'S CHANGEMASTERS

The Tzaangor Shaman Zyclaw leads an army of arcane warriors known as the Changemasters. They roam the Mortal Realms, some to learn from their master, some because they are bound to his service. Those who oppose them are horribly changed – and will perhaps even join Zyclaw's horde as a result.

The Tzaangor Shaman Zyclaw is a bitter and power-hungry soul. Fiercely adamant that the Tzaangors are most favoured of all Tzeentch's worshippers, he likes nothing more than to prove his superiority over the magic users of other races. Since the beginning of his self-imposed quest to locate and destroy nine hundred and ninety-nine other magic users in the name of Tzeentch, his entourage of Tzaangors, Skyfires and Enlightened has been joined by a large number of Kairic Acolytes. The fact that so many human adepts seek to learn at his cloven feet has only bolstered Zyclaw's conviction that he is a true child of Tzeentch. The presence of Mindgouge the

Ogroid Thaumaturge and the Magister Marathyar Vexh has further cemented that claim in Zyclaw's mind, for he has conveniently forgotten the fact he has promised to pay them handsomely for their services.

The Great Architect is most pleased by Zyclaw's vaunting ambition, and has sent a large war party of Horrors to fight at his side. These are the least of the magical monstrosities in the Changemasters' ranks. A pack of Flamers and the Burning Chariot of Cindertongue form the vanguard, turning the gravest enemy threats to multicoloured cinders. Since the Night of the Ritual Knives, where Zyclaw turned an orruk horde into mewling beastmen and sacrificed them on an altar of jade, Archaon has sent the Gaunt Summoner known as the Eater of Tomes to oversee his progress. That in itself is a signal honour, but the pride of Zyclaw's host are the Lords of Change that act as his advisors. In truth, Athata'gryllian of the Cobalt Staff is only there as Kairos Fateweaver's link to the present, and Kairos himself only pretends to serve Zyclaw's interests – in reality the reverse is true. Nonetheless, Tzeentch finds Zyclaw's pyrotechnic displays of dominance to be most entertaining, and never tires of seeing his Shaman's power lay low those who fail to pay him obeisance.

TIDES OF
CHANGE

FORCES OF TZEENTCH

On the following pages, you will find exciting rules for your armies of Tzeentch daemons and Tzeentch Arcanites. These include powerful allegiance abilities, warscrolls and warscroll battalions that describe the arcane forces of Tzeentch for you to use in games of *Warhammer Age of Sigmar*.

ALLEGIANCE ABILITIES

From the deadliest sorceries to esoteric artefacts of incredible power, this section provides rules and abilities for Tzeentch armies, mortal and daemon alike.

ALLEGIANCE

Every unit and warscroll battalion in *Warhammer Age of Sigmar* owes allegiance to one of the Grand Alliances – either Order, Chaos, Death or Destruction. Many units and warscroll battalions also have a more specific allegiance, for example, Tzeentch. If all the starting units and warscroll battalions in your army follow Tzeentch – including any units that you assign the Tzeentch keyword to during set-up – then your army has the Tzeentch allegiance.

An army with the Tzeentch allegiance – sometimes known as a Tzeentch army – can use the potent allegiance abilities found on the following pages.

When your army qualifies for more than one allegiance – e.g. all of the units are Tzeentch and Chaos – you must choose which allegiance your army will use before each game. These restrictions aside, you can use allegiance abilities whenever you play games of *Warhammer Age of Sigmar*.

Battle Traits: An allied army fights with unity and cohesion, granting it additional boons. See the next page for the battle traits available to TZEENTCH armies.

Command Traits: Each leader has their own style of command. See pages 74-75 for the command traits available to TZEENTCH generals.

Artefacts of Power & Daemonic Gifts: Artefacts of power are deadly treasures, borne to war by the mightiest heroes. Similarly, daemonic gifts are unique blessings bestowed by Tzeentch himself upon his most favoured children. You can use the tables in this book to determine which magical artefacts the HEROES from your army can possess.

Spell Lores: The champions of Tzeentch have ever been feared for their mastery of the sorcerous arts. WIZARDS from your army gain a spell from one of two spell lores – the Lore of Fate or the Lore of Change – depending on whether they are a mortal sorcerer or one of Tzeentch's daemons.

NAMED CHARACTERS

Kairos Fateweaver, the Changeling and the Blue Scribes are unique and devastatingly dangerous daemons with their own unique personalities and bespoke items of terrifying power. As such, these models cannot have a command trait or artefact of power.

BATTLEPLANS

Tzeentch's followers have their own unique methods and tactics in war – the battles they fight are unlike those of any other army. The battleplans on pages 84-87 allow you to wage war as the Architect of Fate wills it.

PATH TO GLORY

On pages 88-93 you will find rules for playing a Path to Glory campaign. These enable you to field your Tzeentch miniatures as a formidable warband, and fight an immersive campaign in which your forces grow stronger with each victory. Included are warband tables to help you collect your army, as well as rewards tables for your champion and their followers.

WARSCROLL BATTALIONS

This section describes formations made up of several units that march to war as one, combining their strengths to gain powerful new abilities. By fielding these formations you can muster an Arcanite Cult or convocation of Tzeentch on the tabletop. There are rules for fielding some of the most renowned cults and convocations, each possessing its own strengths and distinct character.

WARSCROLLS

This section describes the characteristics and abilities of the individual Tzeentch daemons and Tzeentch Arcanite models and units.

ALLEGIANCE ABILITIES

A Tzeentch army is a truly maddening sight, hordes of gibbering daemons, multihued mutants and masked cultists marching forth to enact the unfathomable will of their dark master. Described below are the battle traits that a Tzeentch army possesses, and the command traits that its general can have.

BATTLE TRAITS

Armies with the TZEENTCH allegiance have the following ability:

Masters of Destiny: To serve the Changer of the Ways is to instinctively understand the ebb and flow of future events, and be able to manipulate their potential to the fullest.

After set-up, but before rolling to see which player takes the first turn in the first battle round, roll 9 dice and keep them to one side; this is your pool of Destiny Dice. Though it is possible for some or even all of these dice to be replenished during the course of the battle, the number of dice in your pool of Destiny Dice can never exceed 9.

Designer's Note: *To avoid inadvertently muddling them up with your other dice, we suggest using D6s of different size, design or colour to represent your Destiny Dice.*

Before rolling any dice for a TZEENTCH unit, you can use one or more of the remaining Destiny Dice from your pool in their stead; the result of the roll you would have made is automatically substituted with the result shown on the Destiny Dice you have chosen to use. For example, instead of rolling a dice to see how far one of your units runs in the movement phase, you could expend a Destiny Dice from your pool

to determine the result automatically – if you expended a Destiny Dice that showed a result of 5, the unit would run 5". Destiny Dice can be expended to fix the result of any of the following nine types of dice rolls:

- Casting roll
- Unbinding roll
- Run roll
- Charge roll
- Hit roll
- Wound roll
- Save roll
- Damage roll
- Battleshock test

Note that each Destiny Dice expended only allows you to substitute a single dice roll. For example, in the case of a charge roll (which requires you to roll two dice), you would need to expend two dice from your pool of Destiny Dice if you wished to predetermine the entire charge distance. You must also use any Destiny Dice you wish to expend before rolling any remaining dice as part of an action. For example, if you were about to make five hit rolls, but wanted to predetermine two of the results by expending Destiny Dice, you must do so immediately, then roll the remaining three dice.

COMMAND TRAITS

In addition to their command abilities, if they are a HERO, the general of a TZEENTCH army can have a command trait from the appropriate list on the page opposite. Depending on whether your general is a DAEMON, an ARCANITE and/or a MORTAL, you can choose a command trait from the Tzeentch Daemons, Tzeentch Arcanites or Tzeentch Mortals Command Trait tables respectively (if they qualify for more than one table, you can pick which one to use). Pick the trait that best suits your general's personality. Alternatively, you can roll a dice to randomly determine a trait. If, for any reason, you must select a new general during a battle, immediately generate a trait for them.

TZEENTCH ARCANITES

D6 Command Trait

1 **Arch-sorcerer:** Generate two additional spells for your general from the Lore of Fate (pg 80).

2 **Nexus of Fate:** If your general is on the battlefield at the start of your hero phase, roll a dice; on a 1 or 6, you can choose to replace one Destiny Dice from your pool with the number you rolled.

3 **Magical Supremacy:** You can attempt to unbind enemy spells with your general that are cast within 27" of them instead of 18".

4 **Boundless Mutation:** At the start of each of your hero phases, roll a dice; on a 2 or more, your general heals D3 wounds. On a roll of 1, your general suffers one mortal wound; if this results in their death, replace your general with a Chaos Spawn under your control.

5 **Cult Demagogue:** Add 2 to the Bravery of all friendly TZEENTCH ARCANITES that are within 9" of your general.

6 **Arcane Sacrifice:** At the start of your hero phase, you can inflict D3 mortal wounds on a friendly unit within 3" of your general. If you do so, then you can re-roll any failed casting rolls for your general for the duration of that phase, and increase the range of any spells they cast by 9".

TZEENTCH DAEMONS

D6 Command Trait

1 **Arch-sorcerer:** Generate two additional spells for your general from the Lore of Change (pg 82).

2 **Nexus of Fate:** If your general is on the battlefield at the start of your hero phase, roll a dice; on a 1 or 6, you can choose to replace one Destiny Dice from your pool with the number you rolled.

3 **Magical Supremacy:** You can attempt to unbind enemy spells with your general that are cast within 27" of them instead of 18".

4 **Daemonspark:** Once per battle, in your hero phase, you can unleash the Daemonspark. Add 1 to the Damage characteristic of all of your general's melee weapons for the rest of the turn.

5 **Incorporeal Form:** Your opponent must subtract 1 from any hit rolls that target your general in the combat phase.

6 **Aether Tether:** You can re-roll save rolls of 1 for your general.

TZEENTCH MORTALS

D6 Command Trait

1 **Arch-sorcerer:** Generate two additional spells for your general from the Lore of Fate (pg 80).

2 **Nexus of Fate:** If your general is on the battlefield at the start of your hero phase, roll a dice; on a 1 or 6, you can choose to replace one Destiny Dice from your pool with the number you rolled.

3 **Magical Supremacy:** You can attempt to unbind enemy spells with your general that are cast within 27" of them instead of 18".

4 **Blessing of Tzeentch:** Each time your general suffers a wound or mortal wound, roll a dice; on a roll of 6, the wound is ignored.

5 **Soul Burn:** Each time you make a wound roll of 6 or higher for any of your general's melee weapons, the target unit suffers 1 mortal wound in addition to any other damage it suffers.

6 **Illusionist:** Your opponent must subtract 1 from any hit rolls that target your general in the shooting phase.

ARTEFACTS OF POWER

These artefacts are shaped by the sorcerers and spellsmiths devoted to Tzeentch. They can be sentient weapons, mutating shields or more esoteric items, but all are potent tools ensorcelled with dark magic.

If a **Tzeentch** army includes any **Arcanite Heroes** or **Mortal Heroes**, then one may bear an artefact of power. Declare which **Hero** has the artefact after picking your general, and then pick which artefact the **Hero** has. Ideally, that artefact should fit the model's appearance or the backstory you have given them. Alternatively, roll a dice on the relevant table on these two pages to randomly select one.

You may choose one additional **Hero** to have an artefact of power for each warscroll battalion in your army. The same model cannot have more than one artefact of power.

TREASURES OF THE CULTS

Any **Arcanite Hero** can be given one of the following treasures of the cults.
A weapon picked to be a treasure of the cults cannot be a weapon used by a mount.

D6 Treasure of the Cults

1 Ambition's End: Many a sorcerer's quest to master the magical arts has ended upon this weapon's blade, for it spills not only blood but knowledge itself.

Pick one of the bearer's melee weapons to be an Ambition's End. Roll a dice at the end of the combat phase for any **Hero** that suffers an unsaved wound from this weapon. On a 5 or 6, they also suffer a mortal wound. If they are a **Wizard**, they also forget a random spell for the rest of the battle.

2 Secret-eater: Should this weapon slay one touched by fate, its bearer inherits a measure of their destiny.

Pick one of the bearer's weapons to be a Secret-eater. Each time a **Hero** is slain by this weapon, you may roll another dice and immediately add it to your pool of Destiny Dice.

3 Spiteful Shield: This shield exemplifies Tzeentch's predilection for cruel twists of fate.

Roll a dice for each successful hit roll made against the bearer in the combat phase. On a 6, the attacking unit suffers a mortal wound once the attack has been resolved.

4 Souldraught: To imbibe this heady brew is to know a fleeting measure of unrivalled power.

Once per battle, in any hero phase, the bearer may drink this potion. Until the end of the phase, roll three dice whenever they attempt to cast or unbind a spell and use the two highest results.

5 Glamour Fetish: Disturbing and unsightly in equal measure, this fetish holds the power to unsettle even the most stoic warrior.

Your opponent must add 1 to the result of any battleshock tests they take for their units within 9" of the bearer.

6 Windthief Charm: Should the bearer activate this talisman's otherworldly enchantment, the mundane power of gravity will hold sway upon them no longer.

Once per battle, you can use the Windthief Charm to move the bearer up to double their Move characteristic. During this move, the bearer can move as if they could fly.

FATED ARTEFACTS

Any **Tzeentch Mortal Hero** can be given one of the following fated artefacts.
A weapon picked to be a fated artefact cannot be a weapon used by a mount.

D6 Fated Artefact

1 Wicked Shard: Empowered by the bearer's sorcerous might, this blade is anathema to life.

Pick one of the bearer's melee weapons to be a Wicked Shard. Re-roll wound rolls of 1 for this weapon. Re-roll all failed wound rolls instead if the bearer successfully cast or unbound a spell in the same turn.

2 Changeblade: To fall to this blade is to be transmuted into a writhing mass of flesh and tentacles.

Pick one of the bearer's melee weapons to be a Changeblade. Whenever a **Hero** is slain by this weapon, replace the slain model with a **Chaos Spawn** under your control. The Chaos Spawn cannot do anything this turn.

3 Nexus Staff: Those slain by this cursed stave have their soul-stuff torn from their bodies to fuel a terrible enchantment upon their former brothers in arms.

Pick one of the bearer's weapons to be a Nexus Staff. Each time a **Hero** is slain by this weapon, you can unleash the soul it has stolen as a burst of power; roll a dice for each enemy unit within 9". On a 4 or more the unit being rolled for suffers D3 mortal wounds.

4 Timeslip Pendant: Time is a mutable concept to the bearer of this amulet.

Once per battle, at the end of any combat phase, the bearer can enter a timeslip. If they do, they can pile in and attack for a second time.

5 Daemonheart: Through a dark ritual, the heart of a daemon dwells within the bearer's chest, where its dread power can be unleashed to greatly augment the strength of its host.

Once per battle, at the end of any hero phase, the bearer can tap into the baleful energies of the Daemonheart. Add 1 to the Damage characteristic of all of the bearer's melee weapons for the duration of the turn. However, at the end of the combat phase, roll a dice; on a roll of 1, the bearer suffers a mortal wound.

6 Paradoxical Shield: This shield exists simultaneously on both the physical and ethereal planes.

Add 2 to any save rolls you make for the bearer. However, you must re-roll all successful save rolls you make for them.

DAEMONIC GIFTS

Daemonic gifts are one with the immortal creatures that bear them, traits intrinsically bound to their essence. They are bestowed by Tzeentch upon only his most favoured servants.

If a TZEENTCH army includes any DAEMON HEROES, then one may bear a daemonic gift. Declare which HERO has the daemonic gift after picking your general, and then pick which gift the HERO has. Ideally, that gift should fit the appearance of the model or the backstory you have given them.

Alternatively, pick one of the tables on these two pages and roll a dice to randomly select one. You may choose one additional DAEMON HERO to have a daemonic gift for each warscroll battalion in your army. The same model cannot have more than one daemonic gift.

If your TZEENTCH army is comprised of any combination of DAEMON, ARCANITE and MORTAL units, daemonic gifts are treated as artefacts of power for the purposes of determining how many you can include in your army.

DAEMONIC WEAPONS

Any TZEENTCH DAEMON HERO can be given one of the following daemonic weapons.
A weapon picked to be a daemonic weapon cannot be one used by a mount.

D6   Daemonic Weapon

1   Warpfire Blade: The flames that flicker around this daemon's blade can ignite the soul of its victim.

Pick one of the bearer's melee weapons to be a Warpfire Blade. Wound rolls of 6 made for this weapon cause a mortal wound in addition to their normal damage.

2   Sentient Weapons: This daemon's armaments seem to be guided by their own, unerring will.

Enemy units can never benefit from modifiers to their save rolls or Save characteristic (e.g. from being in cover) against attacks made by this daemon.

3   Blade of Fate: This daemon-blade will serve its master well – if they can tame the vagaries of fate.

Pick one of the bearer's melee weapons to be a Blade of Fate. If you have at least one dice in your pool of Destiny Dice when making an attack with this weapon, you can re-roll failed hit and wound rolls of 1. However, if there are 9 Destiny Dice in the pool when the bearer attacks with this weapon, you can instead re-roll all failed hit and wound rolls.

4   Souleater: This evil blade grows stronger as it gluts itself upon souls of sufficient worth.

Pick one of the bearer's melee weapons to be a Souleater. Each time the bearer slays a HERO with this weapon, add 1 to this weapon's Attacks for the rest of the battle.

5   Phantasmal Weapons: This daemon's strikes can pass through armour to cleave the flesh beneath.

Improve the Rend characteristic of all melee weapons wielded by this daemon by 1 (if it has a Rend characteristic of '-' it becomes -1).

6   Pyrofyre Stave: This ornate staff is wreathed in flickering warpflame, and any aetheric fire channelled through it burns with even greater fury.

Add 1 to any wound rolls you make for the bearer's attacks in the shooting phase.

DAEMONIC POWERS

Any **Tzeentch Daemon Hero** can be given one of the following daemonic powers.

D6 Daemonic Power

1 Lord of Flux: This daemon's essence is an affront to existence; its mere presence can see foes torn apart as reality itself twists and buckles in torment around it.

Roll a dice at the beginning of each combat phase for each enemy unit within 3" of this daemon. On a roll of 4 or more that unit suffers a mortal wound.

2 Aura of Mutability: Even the slightest injury serves as an opportunity for bountiful change in close proximity to this daemon.

You can re-roll wound rolls of 1 for friendly units of **Tzeentch Daemons** within 3" of this daemon.

3 Cursed Ichor: In place of blood, baleful fluids erupt forth from this daemon's wounds, dousing its would-be killers with tainted vitae.

Roll a dice after any wounds are inflicted upon this daemon. On a roll of 2 or more, one enemy model within 1" of them suffers 1 mortal wound. If several enemy models are within range, randomly determine which one suffers the mortal wound.

4 Wellspring of Arcane Might: This daemon is a living font of sorcerous energy, which his minions can draw upon to fuel their own spells.

You can re-roll any casting roll dice which are showing a 1 for any friendly units of **Tzeentch Daemons** within 9" of this daemon.

5 Aspect of Tzeentch: To know even a fraction of the Architect of Fate's power is to know the boundless possibilities of destiny and how best to manipulate it.

Each time you expend a Destiny Dice whilst this daemon is on the battlefield, roll a dice. On a 6 you may immediately roll another dice and add it to your Destiny Dice pool.

6 Mark of the Conjurer: This daemon has an intrinsic gift to find flaws in the physical plane which its kin can more easily breach when called upon to do so.

When attempting to summon a **Tzeentch Daemon** unit with this daemon, add 1 to the casting roll.

THE LORE OF FATE

The spell lore of the mortal followers of Tzeentch centres around cunning, manipulation and trickery – those proficient in its use inevitably rise high in the Great Schemer's favour.

Each **Arcanite Wizard** and **Mortal Wizard** in a **Tzeentch** army knows an additional spell chosen from the Lore of the Fate. This treacherous magic allows these ambitious individuals to manipulate fate to their advantage – so far as they can predict it. Pick one that best matches the background story of your wizard. Alternatively, you can roll a dice to randomly determine which extra spell is known to the wizard.

Note that each **Wizard** in a **Tzeentch** army can know a different spell. If you prefer, you can instead generate (pick or roll) one spell that will be known by all your **Tzeentch Arcanite Wizards** and/or **Tzeentch Mortal Wizards**.

1. BOLT OF TZEENTCH

This spell manifests as a prismatic beam of raw magic that tortures reality at its passing, tearing its victims apart in a spectacular display of multispectral colour.

Bolt of Change has a casting value of 8. If successfully cast, pick a visible enemy unit within 18" of the caster. The unit you pick suffers D6 mortal wounds.

2. ARCANE SUGGESTION

Overwhelming reason with magical force of will, the sorcerer's victims are reduced to little more than puppets on a string.

Arcane Suggestion has a casting value of 7. If successfully cast, choose an enemy unit (but not a **Hero** or **Monster**) within 18", roll a dice and consult the following table:

D3	Result
1	**It's Hopeless:** The unit immediately suffers D3 mortal wounds.
2	**Drop Your Weapons:** Until the end of this turn, subtract 1 from hit and wound rolls for the unit.
3	**Turn Around:** Until the end of this turn, subtract 1 from save rolls for the unit.

3. GLIMPSE THE FUTURE

By focussing on the skeins of potential fates, the sorcerer gleans a hint of future events in time to manipulate them to his advantage.

Glimpse the Future has a casting value of 7. Only one of your **Wizards** can attempt to cast this spell per turn. If successfully cast, roll a dice and add it to your Destiny Dice pool.

4. SHIELD OF FATE

There is little better protection than to be guided by destiny itself, protected by the very hand of fate.

Shield of Fate has a casting value of 5. If successfully cast, pick a friendly **Tzeentch** unit within 18" of the caster. Until the start of your next hero phase, you can re-roll save rolls of 1 for the unit if you have 1-3 Destiny Dice, save rolls of 1 and 2 if you have 4-6 Destiny Dice, or save rolls of 1, 2 and 3 if you have 7-9 Destiny Dice. The dice results you can re-roll will change accordingly if any Destiny Dice are added to or expended from your pool.

5. INFUSION ARCANUM

Channelling their arcane might inwards, the sorcerer's body becomes saturated with death-dealing energies, transforming even the frailest warlock into a truly formidable adversary.

Infusion Arcanum has a casting value of 5. If successfully cast, until your next hero phase you can add 1 to all hit and wound rolls for the caster.

6. TREACHEROUS BOND

By creating a psycho-conductive link, the sorcerer can siphon the worst of any harm that befalls them and channel it to the unsuspecting brethren with whom they have magically bound themselves.

Treacherous Bond has a casting value of 6. If successfully cast, pick a visible friendly unit within 18" of the caster. Until your next hero phase, so long as the bonded unit is within 9" of the caster, roll a dice whenever the caster suffers an unsaved wound or mortal wound; on a 2 or more the chosen unit suffers the wound or mortal wound instead.

THE LORE OF CHANGE

The daemons of Tzeentch wield the raw stuff of change, the very essence of what is known as magic. So dangerous is this form of sorcery that mortal conjurers could not hope to control its baleful energies.

Each **Daemon Wizard** in a **Tzeentch** army knows an additional spell chosen from the Lore of Change. This unpredictable, powerful magic allows these daemons to channel the reality-bending powers of Tzeentch. Pick one that best matches the background story or convocation of your wizard. Alternatively, you can roll a dice to randomly determine which extra spell is known to the wizard.

Note that each **Wizard** in a **Tzeentch** army can know a different spell. If you prefer, you can instead generate (pick or roll) one spell that will be known by all your **Tzeentch Daemon Wizards**.

1. BOLT OF TZEENTCH

This spell manifests as a prismatic beam of raw magic that tortures reality at its passing, tearing its victims apart in a spectacular display of multispectral colour.

Bolt of Change has a casting value of 8. If successfully cast, pick a visible enemy unit within 18" of the caster. The unit you pick suffers D6 mortal wounds.

2. TREASON OF TZEENTCH

Tzeentch delights in sowing treachery and deceit, and many of his daemonic sorcerers can channel this aspect of their master's power to set brother upon brother.

Treason of Tzeentch has a casting value of 5. If successfully cast, pick a visible enemy unit within 18" of the caster. One model in the unit you pick immediately attacks the rest of the unit as if it were the combat phase, using whichever weapons you choose. However, a model will never attack itself as a result of this spell, so it can only affect a unit that has more than one model.

3. ARCANE TRANSFORMATION

Many of Tzeentch's servants bear the gift of mutation, and this daemon can call upon its master to bestow just such a blessing.

Arcane Transformation has a casting value of 7. If successfully cast, pick a visible friendly **Hero** within 18" of the caster. You can permanently increase that model's Move, Bravery or the Attacks characteristic of one of its weapons by 1. However, each **Hero** can only be chosen as the target of this spell once per battle.

4. UNCHECKED MUTATION

Those touched by this mutagenic spell are either forced to evolve at such a ferocious rate that their bodies are torn apart by the trauma of such rapid physical change, or suffer spontaneous hyper-devolution into an indescribable mass of primordial ooze.

Unchecked Mutation has a casting value of 7. If successfully cast, pick a visible enemy unit within 18" of the caster. The unit you pick suffers D3 mortal wounds and then you roll a dice; on a roll of 5 or 6 the unit suffers another mortal wound and you roll another dice as above.

5. FOLD REALITY

Reality is but another plaything for the daemons of Tzeentch. This spell holds the power to undo and remake existence at will, though doing so is never without its risks…

Fold Reality has a casting value of 7. If successfully cast, pick a visible friendly unit of **Tzeentch Daemons** within 18" of the caster and roll a dice. On a roll of 2 or more, you can return that many slain models to the unit. On a roll of 1, the unit is wiped out!

6. TZEENTCH'S FIRESTORM

An apocalyptic inferno of raging warpflame surges forth from the daemon's outstretched hands to engulf its victims in a fiery maelstrom.

Tzeentch's Firestorm has a casting value of 9. If successfully cast, pick a visible enemy unit within 18" of the caster. Roll 9 dice – for each 6 that you roll the unit you picked suffers D3 mortal wounds.

BANQUET OF MAGIC

HOW TO USE BATTLEPLANS

This book contains two battleplans, each of which enables you to fight a battle that epitomises the way the Disciples of Tzeentch go to war. These battles should be fought using all of the rules on the *Warhammer Age of Sigmar* rules sheet unless the battleplan specifically indicates otherwise. Each of the battleplans includes a map reflecting the landscape on which the battle is fought; these maps usually show a battlefield that is 6 feet by 4 feet in size, but you can use a smaller or larger area if you wish.

More so than those of the other Dark Gods are Tzeentch's daemons invigorated in the presence of arcane power. Should such magics be freed from their confinement, the power of Tzeentch's legions will reach terrifying new heights of potency.

THE ARMIES

One player commands an army of Tzeentch daemons and their opponent commands the land's occupiers, who are jealously guarding the sorcerous wards that protect their territory.

TZEENTCH DAEMON PLAYER'S OBJECTIVES

Great Tzeentch has led you to these lands, for they are rich in sorcerous power for you to plunder. March forth and free the magic that your enemies have foolishly shackled, and use the unbound energies to punish them for their folly.

OCCUPIER'S OBJECTIVES

A horde of Tzeentch's daemons approaches your lands, intent upon draining the sorcerous wards that protect your people and using their power to secure your demise. Hold them back at all costs, or all will be lost.

THE BATTLEFIELD

The battlefield represents the outskirts of a settlement that shelters a network of defensive enchantments invisible to the naked eye. To the army of Tzeentch daemons that descends upon it, however, the magic that fuels the wards shines like a beacon.

First of all, the occupier places six terrain features, one in each 2' by 2' area of the battlefield, to contain the sorcerous wards that protect their land. Players can then choose to set up any remaining scenery as described on the *Warhammer Age of Sigmar* rules sheet, or use the example scenery shown on the map below.

SORCEROUS WARDS

A network of sorcerous wards protects the settlement beyond, not only empowering its defenders, but serving as a last line of defence that they refuse to yield without a fight.

If a piece of scenery contains a sorcerous ward that has not yet been unbound (see Unbinding the Wards on the next page), all of the occupier's units that are within 3" of it are shielded and filled with determination to defend it. Roll a dice each time a model from such a unit suffers a wound or mortal wound. On a 6 that wound is ignored. In addition, the occupier can choose to re-roll battleshock tests for any of their units that are within 3" of a piece of scenery containing a sorcerous ward.

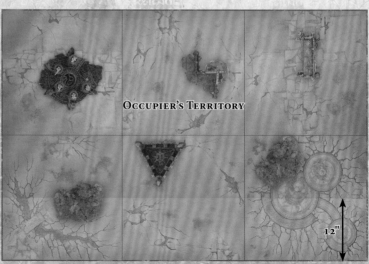

OCCUPIER'S TERRITORY

12"

SOUTHERN BATTLEFIELD EDGE

SET-UP

The occupier sets up all their units first, anywhere that is more than 12" from the southern edge of the battlefield (see map). The Tzeentch daemons player does not set up any of their models yet, but moves them on from the southern edge of the battlefield as part of their move in the first turn of the battle.

FIRST TURN

The Tzeentch daemons player takes the first turn in the first battle round.

UNBINDING THE WARDS

Should the Tzeentch daemons overrun a site containing a sorcerous ward, they will free the magical power stored within, and in doing so saturate the air with aetheric energies. If a Tzeentch daemons unit ends its turn within 3" of a terrain piece containing a sorcerous ward, and no units belonging to the occupier are within 3" of that terrain, the sorcerous ward

is unbound (see Victory on the right, and Sorcerous Wards on the previous page). Each sorcerous ward can only be unbound once during the battle.

Consult the table below each time a sorcerous ward is unbound. Depending on how many sorcerous wards they have successfully unbound, the following cumulative effects apply to the Tzeentch daemons player for the rest of the battle:

Wards Unbound	Effect
1	Add 1 to any unbinding rolls you make.
2	Add 1 to any casting rolls you make.
3	Re-roll all save rolls of 1.
4	Re-roll all hit rolls of 1.
5	Re-roll all wound rolls of 1.

VICTORY

Do not use any of the victory conditions on the *Warhammer Age of Sigmar* rules sheet. If a player has no models on the battlefield at the end of a battle round, the battle ends and their opponent wins a **major victory**. Alternatively, if the Tzeentch daemons player successfully unbinds all six sorcerous wards, the battle ends and they win a **major victory**. Otherwise the battle lasts for five battle rounds.

If, at the end of the fifth battle round, the Tzeentch daemons have unbound fewer than four sorcerous wards, the occupier wins a **major victory**; if four sorcerous wards have been unbound, the result is a **draw**. If more than four sorcerous wards have been unbound, the Tzeentch daemons player wins a **major victory**.

THE SKEINS OF FATE

When the Arcanite Cults reveal themselves and march to war, they do so in the surety of knowledge that they serve some aspect of their master's purpose. Yet despite a cult's determination to enact Tzeentch's will, the plans of the Great Conspirator are rarely obvious at first, even to those that carry them out. However, the cult's leaders are masters of reading even the subtlest signs proffered to them by the Changer of the Ways, and can decipher what Tzeentch requires of them even in the heat of battle.

THE ARMIES

One player commands an army of Tzeentch Arcanites and their opponent's army is made up of the region's inhabitants against which the Tzeentchian cult has revealed its sudden treachery.

TZEENTCH ARCANITE PLAYER'S OBJECTIVES

Lord Tzeentch has given his blessing for you to rise up and slay his enemies, though the details of his Great Plan have yet to be revealed to you. Take the fight to the foe and have faith that your god's will shall soon become clear.

INHABITANT'S OBJECTIVES

An insidious Arcanite Cult has at last revealed itself, and now faces you in open battle. Put them down without mercy before they can achieve their undoubtedly nefarious goal.

PUTTING DOWN THE CULT

The inhabitant earns 2 Laurels of Victory each time they wipe out a unit belonging to the Tzeentch Arcanite player. However, if they slay one of the cult's leaders (a **HERO** belonging to the Tzeentch Arcanite player), the inhabitant earns 3 Laurels of Victory instead.

TZEENTCH'S WILL REVEALED

At the start of each battle round, before rolling to see which player takes the first turn, the Tzeentch Arcanite player must roll a dice and consult the 'Tzeentch's Will' table on the next page to discover what deeds Tzeentch requires the cult to perform, and how the Tzeentch Arcanite player can earn Laurels of Victory.

TZEENTCH ARCANITE PLAYER'S TERRITORY

INHABITANT'S TERRITORY

12"

THE BATTLEFIELD

The Arcanite Cult has chosen this place to reveal itself, drawing those they seek to overthrow towards a battleground of their choosing.

The Tzeentch Arcanite player can set up any three terrain features anywhere on the battlefield. The players can either generate any remaining scenery for this battle as described on the *Warhammer Age of Sigmar* rules sheet, or use the example scenery shown on the map.

SET-UP

Starting with the Tzeentch Arcanite player, each player takes it in turns to set up their units, as described on the *Warhammer Age of Sigmar* rules sheet. Models must be set up in their own territory as shown on the map.

FIRST TURN

The Tzeentch Arcanite player decides who takes the first turn in the first battle round.

VICTORY

Do not use any of the victory conditions on the *Warhammer Age of Sigmar* rules sheet. If a player has no models on the battlefield at the end of a battle round, the battle ends and their opponent wins a **major victory**. Otherwise, the battle lasts for five battle rounds. The player that has earned the most Laurels of Victory (see Tzeentch's Will Revealed on the previous page) by the end of the fifth battle round wins a **major victory**.

D3	Tzeentch's Will
1	**Magical Dominance:** Earn 1 Laurel of Victory each time you successfully cast a spell, or successfully unbind a spell cast by an enemy wizard, during the battle round.
2	**Ritual Slaughter:** Earn 1 Laurel of Victory for every 9 enemy models that are removed (slain or fled) during the battle round.
3	**Glory to Tzeentch!:** Earn 2 Laurels of Victory each time an enemy unit is wiped out during the battle round. Earn 3 Laurels of Victory instead each time an enemy HERO is slain during the battle round.

PATH TO GLORY CAMPAIGNS

Path to Glory campaigns centre around collecting and fighting battles with a warband in the Age of Sigmar. Champions fight each other and gather followers to join them in their quest for glory, taking advantage of this age of unending battle to win great renown.

In order to take part in a Path to Glory campaign, you will need two or more players. All players will need to have at least one **Hero**, who is their champion, and must then create a warband to follow and fight beside their champion during the campaign.

The players fight battles against each other using the warbands they have created. The results of these battles will gain their warband favour. The warband will swell in numbers as more warriors flock to their banner, while existing troops become more powerful.

After gaining enough favour in the eyes of your patron, your champion will be granted a final test. Succeed at the test, and your champion's glory will be affirmed for all time, and you will be crowned as the victor of the campaign.

CREATING A WARBAND

When creating a Path to Glory warband, do not select your army in the normal manner. Instead, your army consists of a mighty **Hero** battling to earn the favour of the gods, and their entire band of loyal followers. As you wage war against other warbands, your own warband will grow, and existing units will become grizzled veterans.

WARBAND ROSTER

The details and progress of each warband need to be recorded on a warband roster, which you can download for free from games-workshop.com.

To create a warband, simply follow these steps and record the results on your warband roster:

1. First, pick an allegiance for your warband. Each allegiance has its own set of warband tables that are used to generate the units in the warband and the rewards they can receive for fighting battles. The warband tables included in this battletome let you collect a warband with the **Tzeentch Arcanite** or **Tzeentch Daemon** allegiance, but other *Warhammer Age of Sigmar* publications include warband tables to let you collect warbands from the grand alliances of **Order**, **Chaos**, **Death** and **Destruction**.

2. Next, choose the champion of your warband by choosing one of the options from your allegiance's champion table. The type of champion you choose will determine the number of rolls you can make for the champion's followers. Give your champion a suitably grand and imposing name, and write this down on your warband roster.

3. Having chosen your champion, the next step is to generate your starting followers. These can be chosen from the followers tables for your allegiance. If your allegiance has more than one followers table you can freely choose which ones you use, selecting all of your followers from a single table or from several. Instead of choosing, you can place your destiny in the hands of fate and roll on the followers tables instead. To make a followers roll, pick a column from one of the followers tables and then roll a dice.

4. Instead of generating a unit of followers, you can choose to gain 1 Glory Point (see page 89). You can sacrifice any number of your starting units of followers in this way. Taking Glory Points instead of a unit makes it easier to gain the 10 points you need to have a chance of winning, but you will have fewer units with which to fight your battles.

5. Your followers need to be organised into units. The follower table tells you how many models the unit has. Follower units cannot include additional models, but they can otherwise take any options listed on their warscroll. **Chaos** warband followers can only be given the mark of their champion's patron. Record all of the information about your followers on your warband roster.

6. Finally, give your warband a name, one that will inspire respect and dread in your rivals. Your warband is now complete, and you can fight your first battle. Good luck!

TO WAR!

Having created a warband, you can now fight battles with it. These battles are fought against other warbands taking part in the campaign.

You can fight battles as and when you wish, and can use any of the battleplans available for *Warhammer Age of Sigmar*. There are some battleplans, for example in the *General's Handbook*, that have been designed specifically for use in Path to Glory campaigns.

The units you use for a game must be those on your warband's roster. Wizards can summon other units during the course of a battle, but they will vanish once the battle is over (wizards belonging to a Chaos warband can only summon the daemons of their patron god). Units can either be fielded at their full roster strength, or broken down into smaller units, as long as no unit is smaller than the minimum size shown on its warscroll.

Any casualties suffered by a warband are assumed to have been replaced in time for its next battle. If your champion is slain in a battle, it is assumed that they were merely injured or knocked out, and they are back to their full fighting strength for your next game, thirsty for vengeance!

GAINING GLORY

All of the players in the campaign are vying for glory. The amount of glory they have received is represented by the Glory Points that the warband has accumulated. Glory can be increased by fighting and winning battles, as described next. As a warband's glory increases, it will also attract additional followers, and a warband's champion may be granted rewards.

Warbands receive Glory Points after a battle is complete. If the warband tied or lost the battle, it receives 1 Glory Point. If it won the battle, it receives D3 Glory Points. You can re-roll a result of 1 on the D3 roll if the warband won a **major victory**.

Add the Glory Points you scored to the total recorded on your roster. Once you have won 10 Glory Points, you will have a chance to win the campaign, as described below.

REWARDS OF BATTLE

Each allegiance has its own set of rewards tables. After each battle you can take one of the three following options. Alternatively, roll a dice to determine which option to take (1-2 = Additional Followers, 3-4 = Champion's Reward, 5-6 = Follower's Reward).

1 **Additional Followers:** More followers flock to your champion's banner. Either select a new unit from one of the follower tables, or roll for a random unit from one of those tables, then add them to your warband roster.

2 **Champion's Reward:** Your champion's prowess continues to grow. Make a roll on the champion rewards table for your allegiance. Make a note of the result on your warband roster. If you roll a result the unit has already received, roll again until you get a different result.

3 **Follower's Reward:** Those who have stood with your champion become renowned for their mighty deeds. Pick a unit in your warband, then make a roll on the followers rewards table for your allegiance. Make a note of the result on your warband roster. If you roll a result the unit has already received, roll again until you get a different result.

ETERNAL GLORY

In order to win the Path to Glory campaign, your champion must first reach 10 Glory Points. You must then fight and win one more battle in order for you to be affirmed amongst the ranks of the immortals and win the Path to Glory campaign. If the next battle you fight is tied or lost, you do not receive any Glory Points – just keep on fighting battles until you either win the campaign… or another player wins first!

You can shorten or lengthen a campaign by lowering or increasing the number of Glory Points a champion must earn. For example, for a shorter campaign, you could say that a champion only needs 5 or 6 Glory Points before fighting their final battle, or for a longer one, say that the demanding gods require them to score 15 or even 20 points!

TZEENTCH WARBAND TABLES

Use the following tables to determine the champion that leads your warband, the followers that make up the units which fight at their side, and the rewards they can receive after battle.

CHAMPION TABLE

Champion	Followers
Lord of Change	3 units
Herald of Tzeentch on Burning Chariot	4 units
Fatemaster	5 units
Gaunt Summoner	5 units
Herald of Tzeentch	5 units
Herald of Tzeentch on Disc	5 units
Magister	5 units
Tzaangor Shaman	5 units

RETINUE FOLLOWERS TABLE

D6	Arcanites	Daemons
1	10 Kairic Acolytes	10 Brimstone Horrors
2	10 Kairic Acolytes	10 Blue Horrors
3	10 Tzaangors	10 Pink Horrors
4	10 Tzaangors	3 Flamers of Tzeentch
5	3 Tzaangor Enlightened	3 Screamers of Tzeentch
6	3 Tzaangor Skyfires	1 Burning Chariot of Tzeentch

HERO FOLLOWERS TABLE

D6	Arcanites	Daemons
1-2	1 Tzaangor Shaman	1 Herald of Tzeentch
2	1 Magister	1 Herald of Tzeentch
3	1 Fatemaster	1 Herald of Tzeentch on Disc
4	1 Curseling, Eye of Tzeentch	1 Herald of Tzeentch on Disc
5	1 Ogroid Thaumaturge	1 Herald of Tzeentch on Burning Chariot

DESIGNER'S NOTE

The Path to Glory rules presented in this book allow you to play an exciting campaign with your friends. You can use the rules exactly as they are laid out here, and fight your way along your path to glory! However, you can instead look at these rules as a framework that you can tinker with however you like, to play the campaign that works best for you and your gaming group.

For example, if you're starting new armies, you might start the campaign with fewer followers – perhaps your general and just two or three other units – that will allow everyone to start playing battles a bit sooner. If, on the other hand, your gaming group is looking for a new challenge, you could decide to generate all followers randomly, taking away the option to choose each unit.

You can take things further – there's nothing to stop you writing your own battleplans to use in your Path to Glory campaigns, or adapting the rules from the *General's Handbook* to play battles with three or more players in your campaign. Equally, while we've said that you can adjust the number of Glory Points you need to win the campaign, you could decide with your gaming group on a completely different way to win the campaign – the victor could be the first player to defeat every other player in the campaign, or the first to amass an army of ten or more units.

Essentially, you should feel free to use these rules in whichever way you and your gaming group agree is best. Your path to glory is limitless!

FOLLOWERS REWARDS TABLE

As your warband progresses along the Path to Glory, it will attract more followers, and especially favoured units will become renowned across the Mortal Realms.

D6 Reward

1 **Sworn Disciples:** Once per battle, in your hero phase, you can declare that this unit will prove their devotion to your champion. You can re-roll any failed wound rolls for the unit for the rest of the turn.

2 **Acolytes of Darkness:** Once per battle, in your hero phase, this unit can enact a dark ritual which shrouds them in shadow. The unit receives the benefit of being in cover until the start of your next turn.

3 **Apostles of the Secret Fire:** Once per battle, in your hero phase, this unit can conjure forth a nova of searing warpflame. Roll a dice for each enemy model that is within 9" of this unit; on a roll of 6, the unit of the model being rolled for suffers 1 mortal wound.

4 **Adepts of the Hidden Path:** Once per battle, in your hero phase, this unit can step through a tear in reality. Remove it from the battlefield and then set it up again anywhere more than 6" from enemy models. This counts as its move in the following movement phase.

5 **Devotees of the Dark Rite:** Once per battle, in your hero phase, you can roll a dice for each model in the unit that has been slain. On a result of 5 or 6, return the model to the unit.

6 **Twice-blessed Followers:** Roll twice on this table and apply both results. Re-roll any duplicates or further rolls of 6.

CHAMPION REWARDS TABLE

As your champion progresses along the Path to Glory, they may be gifted with great rewards by their dark patron… if they are deemed worthy.

2D6 Result

2 What the Gods Give…: Your champion has offended their patron and is punished accordingly. Lose D3 Glory Points (to a minimum of 0), and remove all rewards your champion has gained from this table so far from your warband roster. If your warband has another Hero, that model now takes charge and becomes your new champion (if you do not have any Heroes, immediately generate one from the hero follower table to become your new champion. Note that you cannot select a Chaos Spawn to be your new champion – re-roll these results if rolling randomly). Write down your new champion's name on your warband roster ready for the next battle. Of course, if your former champion was a Mortal or Arcanite, they may still have their uses – you may immediately add a Chaos Spawn to your warband as a follower.

3 Unstable Mutation: Roll a dice for the champion in each of your hero phases. On a roll of 1, the champion suffers a mutating spasm and falls writhing to the ground. They cannot move, attack, cast spells or use any abilities until your next hero phase. On a roll of 4 or more, they are filled with the power of Chaos. You can re-roll hit and wound rolls of 1 for the champion until your next hero phase.

4 Acidic Blood: Roll a dice after any wounds are inflicted upon the champion. On a roll of 2 or more, one enemy model within 1" of the champion suffers 1 mortal wound. If several enemy models are within range, randomly determine which one suffers the mortal wound.

5 Ensorcelled Weapon: Pick one weapon used by your champion (it cannot be a weapon used by a mount if they have one). The Rend characteristic of that weapon is improved by 1 (for example, a Rend characteristic of -1 becomes -2 instead).

6 Trickster: Your opponent must subtract 1 from any hit rolls directed at your champion in the shooting phase.

7 Patronage of Tzeentch (Lesser Reward): Your champion gains a reward generated from the lesser reward of Tzeentch table opposite.

8 Patronage of Tzeentch (Greater Reward): Your champion gains a reward generated from the greater reward of Tzeentch table opposite.

9 Patronage of Tzeentch (Exalted Reward): Your champion gains a reward generated from the exalted reward of Tzeentch table opposite.

10 Daemonic Armour: You can re-roll failed save rolls for your champion.

11 Gift of Foresight: Roll a dice each time your champion suffers an unsaved wound or mortal wound; on a roll of 6, the wound is ignored.

12 Twice-blessed Champion: Roll twice on this table and apply both results. Re-roll any duplicates, rolls of 2 and further rolls of 12.

PATRONAGE OF TZEENTCH TABLES

If you roll a Patronage of Tzeentch result on the champion rewards table, generate a reward from the appropriate table below that matches the extent of Tzeentch's favour.

LESSER REWARD OF TZEENTCH TABLE

D3 Result

1 Moment of Destiny: After set-up, but before rolling to see which player has the first turn in the first battle round, roll one dice and place it to one side. You can expend this dice at any point during the battle as if it were a Destiny Dice (see Masters of Destiny, pg 74). However, this Destiny Dice can only be used to fix one of your champion's rolls.

2 Prescience: You can re-roll failed hit rolls of 1 for your champion.

3 Arcane Vessel: Your champion immediately heals 1 wound each time they, or a friendly model within 3" of them, successfully cast a spell (whether it is unbound or not). In addition, your champion heals 1 wound if they are affected by any spell (whether cast by friend or foe). The wound is healed after any effects of the spell have been resolved.

GREATER REWARD OF TZEENTCH TABLE

D3 Result

1 Arcane Knowledge: Add 1 to any casting and unbinding rolls you make for your champion. If your champion is not a WIZARD, treat this result as Magebane (below) instead.

2 Magebane: You can re-roll all failed hit rolls for attacks made by your champion that target enemy WIZARDS.

3 Warpcraft: In your hero phase, you can remove your champion from the battlefield and then set them up again anywhere more than 6" from enemy models. This counts as their move in the following movement phase.

EXALTED REWARD OF TZEENTCH TABLE

D3 Result

1 Fate-cheater: Roll a dice after your first failed save roll for your champion, or when they suffer their first mortal wound; on a roll of 2 or more the wound is ignored.

2 Wreathed in Warpfire: Add 1 to the Damage characteristic of all of your champion's melee weapons.

3 Secrets of Sorcery: Your champion can attempt to cast 1 extra spell in each of your hero phases, and attempt to unbind 1 extra spell in each enemy hero phase. If your champion is not a WIZARD, they become a WIZARD instead! They can attempt to cast 1 spell in each of your own hero phases, and attempt to unbind 1 spell in each enemy hero phase. They know the Arcane Bolt and Mystic Shield spells.

COLLECTING A TZEENTCH ARMY

Having pored over the rich background and gorgeous artwork in this book, by now you are no doubt keen to start mustering your own Tzeentchian army, if you haven't already. This section of the battletome will provide information and guidance for doing just that.

One of the great things about collecting Citadel Miniatures is that there are so many ways to start new collections and add to existing ones. For many people, the miniatures themselves are their inspiration, and you could do a lot worse than following your instincts and just starting with whichever models you find the most appealing. Are you blown away by the Lord of Change? Pick one up and get painting! Did the pictures of bestial Tzaangors or clandestine Kairic Acolytes make you want some of your own? If so, that's your starting point. Collecting miniatures that really excite you will make assembling and painting them that much more compelling and enjoyable.

The same goes for how you paint them. Some collectors just choose their favourite colours and paint their models accordingly. Others will decide to use hues and iconography they've seen in books like this one, or in *White Dwarf* magazine, and replicate those. Whatever you choose to do, your paint scheme will unify your collection and represent its unique character and identity, whether the models are in pride of place on a cabinet shelf or rampaging across the tabletop. Whatever the case, a fully painted collection of Citadel Miniatures is a truly satisfying spectacle of which you can be rightly proud.

The Arcanite Cults each have their own colours and markings. On pages 26 and 27 you will find a selection of Tzeentch's followers from the different cults to inspire your own collection, from the mutation-worshipping Cult of the Transient Form to the warpflame-obsessed Pyrofane Cult. On pages 14 and 24, you will also find symbols of some of the mightiest daemon convocations and cults.

Another source of inspiration for many collectors is the rich background presented throughout our range of *Warhammer Age of Sigmar* books. Perhaps your imagination was sparked by the tale of the Changeling's duplicitous actions, or perhaps you want to delve further into the story of the Arcanite Cults that have infiltrated the twin city of Hammerhal. Maybe another narrative occurred to you, all of your own? All you need is an idea to get started, and there are few things more gratifying than growing a collection based around the story of your army. This can even be carried over onto gaming boards and themed terrain, adding yet another level of dynamism to your collection.

Of course, if an army is meant for one thing, it's war, and the forces of Tzeentch are no strangers to bringing ruination to the civilisations of the Mortal Realms. They are endlessly varied, for Tzeentch's domain is the power of change and infinite possibilities, which offers countless different ways to arrange your models for battle. Throughout this battletome is a wealth of information on the myriad factions of Tzeentch's followers. You can use this directly, or as a starting point for the structure your own army will adopt, be it a small number of Kairic Acolytes tasked with assassinating a prying Lord-Veritant, or a cavorting mass of Horrors and Flamers intent on bringing the fires of change to a sylvaneth wood.

If you want to get the dice rolling and play some games with your Tzeentch collection, the warscroll battalions found on pages 96-111 of this book will be particularly helpful. Each one represents a different element of a cult or convocation, and provides an easy-to-follow guide to collecting a formation. An army is more than the sum of its parts, and these battalions represent the synergy of units working in concert by granting them powerful abilities that reflect their role within the wider army. Using warscroll battalions to build your collection provides escalating benefits and great satisfaction. Each battalion that you complete is its own force, and helps your collection grow into an army worthy of the Great Conspirator.

WARSCROLL BATTALIONS

The warriors of the Mortal Realms often fight in battalions. Each of these deadly fighting formations consists of several units that are organised and trained to fight alongside each other. The units in warscroll battalions can employ special tactics on the battlefield, making them truly deadly foes.

If you wish, you can organise the units in your army into a warscroll battalion. Doing so will give you access to additional abilities that can be used by the units in the battalion. The information needed to use these powerful formations can be found on the warscroll battalion sheets that we publish for *Warhammer Age of Sigmar*. Each warscroll battalion sheet lists the units that make it up, and the rules for any additional abilities that units from the warscroll battalion can use.

When you are setting up, you can set up all of the units in a warscroll battalion instead of setting up a single unit. Alternatively, you can set up some of the units from a warscroll battalion, and set up any remaining units individually later on, or you can set up all of the units individually. For example, in a battle where each player takes it in turns to set up one unit, you could set up one, some or all of the units belonging to a warscroll battalion in your army.

On the following pages you will find a selection of warscroll battalions. Usually, a unit can only belong to one battalion, and so can only benefit from a single set of battalion abilities. However, some very large battalions include other, smaller battalions, and in this case it is possible for a unit to benefit from the abilities of two different battalions at the same time.

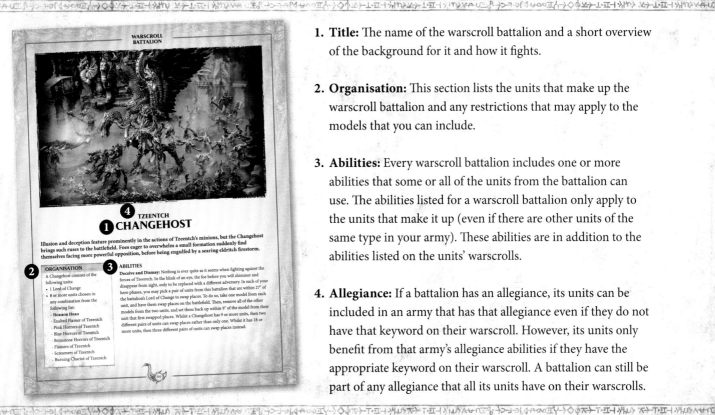

1. **Title:** The name of the warscroll battalion and a short overview of the background for it and how it fights.

2. **Organisation:** This section lists the units that make up the warscroll battalion and any restrictions that may apply to the models that you can include.

3. **Abilities:** Every warscroll battalion includes one or more abilities that some or all of the units from the battalion can use. The abilities listed for a warscroll battalion only apply to the units that make it up (even if there are other units of the same type in your army). These abilities are in addition to the abilities listed on the units' warscrolls.

4. **Allegiance:** If a battalion has an allegiance, its units can be included in an army that has that allegiance even if they do not have that keyword on their warscroll. However, its units only benefit from that army's allegiance abilities if they have the appropriate keyword on their warscroll. A battalion can still be part of any allegiance that all its units have on their warscrolls.

TZEENTCH

WARPFLAME HOST

On the battlefield it is difficult to see a Warpflame Host, for their numbers are concealed behind blazing curtains of Tzeentchian wyrdfire. The intense heat which they give off causes the very air to smoulder as the Warpflame Host unleashes the all-consuming fires of change upon the foe.

ORGANISATION

A Warpflame Host consists of the following units:

- 1 Exalted Flamer of Tzeentch
- 3 or more units chosen in any combination from the following list:
  - Exalted Flamers of Tzeentch
  - Flamers of Tzeentch
  - Burning Chariots of Tzeentch

ABILITIES

Storm of Daemonic Fire: So great is the roiling tide of warpfire surrounding a Warpflame Host that to merely stand in close proximity to the daemons is to risk being set alight. In each of your hero phases, roll a dice for each enemy unit that is within 9" of a unit from a Warpflame Host. On a roll of a 6, the unit being rolled for suffers D3 mortal wounds.

TZEENTCH
MULTITUDINOUS HOST

The Multitudinous Host is a glowing Horror-tide that seeks to drown the foe beneath their multihued numbers. Packed together in one large cavorting mass, the concentration of fate-altering magic is so great that even more Horrors spontaneously burst into existence amongst the cackling throng.

ORGANISATION

A Multitudinous Host consists of the following units:

- 1 Herald of Tzeentch
- 8 or more units chosen in any combination from the following list:
  - Pink Horrors of Tzeentch
  - Blue Horrors of Tzeentch
  - Brimstone Horrors of Tzeentch

ABILITIES

Horrors Without Number: So concentrated is the change-magic that swirls about a Multitudinous Host that the Horrors multiply at an alarming rate. In each of your hero phases, add D6 models to each unit of Pink Horrors and/or Blue Horrors, and add D3 models to each unit of Brimstone Horrors in this battalion.

TZEENTCH
AETHER-EATER HOST

Many of Tzeentch's daemons hunger for magic, coveting the very stuff from which they are forged. In battle the fast-moving Aether-eater Host seeks enemy spellcasters, hoping to leech and absorb the foe's eldritch force and use it to increase their own power.

ORGANISATION

An Aether-eater Host consists of the following units:

- 1 Herald of Tzeentch on Burning Chariot
- 3 or more units chosen in any combination from the following list:
  - The Blue Scribes
  - Herald of Tzeentch on Burning Chariot
  - Herald of Tzeentch on Disc
  - Screamers of Tzeentch

ABILITIES

Feed on Magic: Though all daemons are manifested from raw magic, those of an Aether-eater Host can drain the sorcerous energies unleashed by their foes to revitalise their physical forms. If a unit from an Aether-eater Host successfully unbinds a spell cast by an enemy model, they immediately heal D3 wounds. Whilst an Aether-eater Host has 9 or more units, then any units of Screamers from the battalion can attempt to unbind one spell in each enemy hero phase in the same manner as a wizard (meaning they can also heal wounds as described above).

TZEENTCH

CHANGEHOST

Illusion and deception feature prominently in the actions of Tzeentch's minions, but the Changehost brings such ruses to the battlefield. Foes eager to overwhelm a small formation suddenly find themselves facing more powerful opposition, before being engulfed by a searing eldritch firestorm.

ORGANISATION

A Changehost consists of the following units:

- 1 Lord of Change
- 8 or more units chosen in any combination from the following list:
  - **HORROR HERO**
  - Exalted Flamers of Tzeentch
  - Pink Horrors of Tzeentch
  - Blue Horrors of Tzeentch
  - Brimstone Horrors of Tzeentch
  - Flamers of Tzeentch
  - Screamers of Tzeentch
  - Burning Chariots of Tzeentch

ABILITIES

Deceive and Dismay: Nothing is ever quite as it seems when fighting against the forces of Tzeentch. In the blink of an eye, the foe before you will shimmer and disappear from sight, only to be replaced with a different adversary. In each of your hero phases, you may pick a pair of units from this battalion that are within 27" of the battalion's Lord of Change to swap places. To do so, take one model from each unit, and have them swap places on the battlefield. Then, remove all of the other models from the two units, and set them back up within 9" of the model from their unit that first swapped places. Whilst a Changehost has 9 or more units, then two different pairs of units can swap places rather than only one. Whilst it has 18 or more units, then three different pairs of units can swap places instead.

TZEENTCH
OVERSEER'S FATE-TWISTERS

Aided by an entourage of powerful daemons known as Fate-twisters, the Overseers read the skeins of destiny to sidestep sword-blows and shift the flight of enemy arrows so they clatter harmlessly away. Guided by such future-sight, the Overseers ensure they fulfil their own crucial part in Tzeentch's plan.

ORGANISATION

An Overseer's Fate-twisters battalion consists of the following units:

- 1 Lord of Change
- 8 or more units chosen in any combination from the following list:
  - Horror Hero
  - Exalted Flamers of Tzeentch
  - Burning Chariots of Tzeentch

ABILITIES

The Will of Tzeentch: The Lords of Change known as the Overseers and their most accomplished lieutenants bear the favour of the Great Conspirator, the better to enact his will in all things. At the start of each of your hero phases, add 1 dice to your Destiny Dice pool whilst at least one model from this battalion is on the battlefield. In addition, you can choose to substitute dice rolls that you have already made with Destiny Dice (rather than substituting them before rolling) whilst this battalion has 9 or more models.

Master of Fate: The Overseers are at the centre of an intricate web of lies and deceit, and are tasked with reading the skeins of fate to ensure the fruition of Tzeentch's multifarious plans. If the Lord of Change from this battalion is on the battlefield, then in each of your hero phases you can choose to re-roll the result of one of the dice in your Destiny Dice pool.

TZEENTCH
OMNISCIENT ORACLES

Through manipulation, Kairos Fateweaver has created the perfect bodyguard – his Omniscient Oracles. This gathering of so much eldritch might can scour the battlefield with sorcery or topple entire kingdoms. Even the other Dark Gods pay heed when the Omniscient Oracles take to the field.

ORGANISATION

The Omniscient Oracles consist of the following units:

- Kairos Fateweaver
- 3 Lords of Change

ABILITIES

Knowledge of Past, Present and Future: Kairos Fateweaver sees both the past and the future, but in sealing a soul-binding pact with the Lords of Change known to their kin as the Allscryers, Kairos has ensured the deeds of the moment are made clear to him as well. You can re-roll any hit, wound, save and run rolls of 1 – as well as any dice rolls of 1 in a charge roll – for models from this battalion.

TZEENTCH
THE ETERNAL CONFLAGRATION

All will burn when the hosts of the Eternal Conflagration arrive on the battlefield. Here is no subterfuge or subtlety, for it is this convocation that Tzeentch sends forth to scour the foe – to blast them with unnatural flames. The Flamers of the Eternal Conflagration burn brightest of all, lighting the horizon like a psychedelic sun. The Lord of Change that commands the Eternal Conflagration holds the title of Radiant Lord, and is tasked with bringing fiery annihilation to those that would thwart the plans of Tzeentch. All must burn before the flames of change.

ORGANISATION

The Eternal Conflagration must contain the following:

- 1 Lord of Change or Overseer's Fate-twisters
- 1 Warpflame Host (must contain at least 6 units)

The Eternal Conflagration may also contain:
- 0-8 warscroll battalions chosen in any combination from the following list:
  - Warpflame Host
  - Aether-eater Host
  - Multitudinous Host
  - Changehost
- Any number of additional TZEENTCH DAEMON units

If the Eternal Conflagration contains the maximum number of battalions, it gains the Destiny Preordained ability (pg 104).

ABILITIES

Pawns of the Radiant Lord: The Flamers of the Eternal Conflagration are extensions of their Overseer's will, and the greater daemon uses them as such, channelling destructive magics through them, regardless of cost, to achieve its own ends. When the Lord of Change that must be taken in this battalion attempts to cast a spell, you can select any Flamer from this battalion to act as the casting model – range, visibility and so on are all measured from that model.

Coruscating Flames: As the many Flamers of the Eternal Conflagration bound and cavort across the battlefield, their fires burn ever brighter, dazzling their foes. Your opponent must subtract 1 from any hit rolls that target units of Flamers and Exalted Flamers of Tzeentch from the Eternal Conflagration in the shooting phase.

TZEENTCH
THE HOSTS DUPLICITOUS

The daemons of the Hosts Duplicitous are masters of illusion and deception. Tzeentch sends forth this convocation's hosts on any number of covert actions, such as affecting secret regime changes or stealthily infiltrating well-guarded places of power. In battle the Hosts Duplicitous utilise spell-generated mirages to bolster their ranks, allowing them to strike indiscriminately while their foes waste efforts fighting mere hallucinations. The Lord of Change that leads the Hosts Duplicitous holds the sinister title of Phantom Lord.

ORGANISATION

The Hosts Duplicitous must contain the following:

- 1 Lord of Change or Overseer's Fate-twisters
- 1 Changehost (must contain at least 3 Horror Heroes)

The Hosts Duplicitous may also contain:
- 0-8 warscroll battalions chosen in any combination from the following list:
  - Warpflame Host
  - Aether-eater Host
  - Multitudinous Host
  - Changehost
- Any number of additional Tzeentch Daemon units

If the Hosts Duplicitous contains the maximum number of battalions, it gains the Destiny Preordained ability (pg 104).

ABILITIES

Glamoursmiths: When a Wizard from this battalion rolls a 1 on any dice as part of a casting roll, count it as a 2 instead.

MAGIC

Wizards belonging to the Hosts Duplicitous know the following spell in addition to any others they know:

SCINTILLATING SIMULACRA

Reality ripples around the daemons' foes, and even should their aim be true, they will merely strike phantasmal after-images of their targets. Scintillating Simulacra has a casting value of 6. If successfully cast, pick an enemy unit within 18" of the caster. Until the start of your next hero phase, any successful hit and wound rolls your opponent makes for the unit you picked automatically fail; conversely, any failed hit and wound rolls your opponent makes for them are automatically successful.

TZEENTCH
ARCANITE CULT

When at last the call for open battle arrives, the full Arcanite Cult strides forth to wage war in the name of their patron. Soon, shrill calls and chanting fill the air as the cult hurls itself into the fray, eager to do their part in Tzeentch's Great Plan, and fate itself twists to favour their cause.

ORGANISATION

An Arcanite Cult consists of the following units and battalions:

- 1 Arcanite Cabal
- 3-9 warscroll battalions chosen in any combination from the following list:
  - Alter-kin Coven
  - Skyshoal Coven
  - Tzaangor Coven
  - Witchfyre Coven
- 0-1 Curseling, Eye of Tzeentch
- 0-1 Gaunt Summoner of Tzeentch
- 0-1 Ogroid Thaumaturge

ABILITIES

Destiny Preordained: When Tzeentch's armies are unleashed in their full might, it is to fulfil a purpose that the Change God has long foreseen. When generating your Destiny Dice pool at the start of the battle, you can choose the results of 3 of the dice before rolling the remaining 6 dice as normal.

Strength in Conviction: Sure in their purpose, Arcanite cultists march to war with unshakable confidence that they are enacting their master's ineffable will. Add 1 to the Bravery of all models in an Arcanite Cult.

TZEENTCH
ARCANITE CABAL

The dark heart of an Arcanite Cult is its cabal. While the master of the cult pulls upon the eldritch might of the group to sway the tides of fate, the sorcerers find their own magics likewise enhanced by the cabal's collective power, allowing them each to cast a veritable hurricane of spells.

ORGANISATION

An Arcanite Cabal consists of the following units:

- 3-9 units chosen in any combination from the following list:
  - Fatemaster
  - Magister
  - Tzaangor Shaman

ABILITIES

Master of the Cult: The cult's master wears Tzeentch's favour like a mantle. After set-up, pick one model from this battalion to be the master of the cult. Each time you use a Destiny Dice to predetermine a dice roll for the master of the cult, roll a dice; on a roll of 4, 5 or 6, you may roll another dice and immediately add it to your Destiny Dice pool.

Cabal of Sorcerers: With their powers combined, the sorcerers of an Arcanite Cabal are far greater than the sum of their parts. Each model from an Arcanite Cabal that is within 9" of at least two other models from the same battalion in your hero phase can attempt to cast one additional spell.

TZEENTCH

ALTER-KIN COVEN

Death is perhaps the most lenient of fates that await those who dare defy an Alter-kin Coven. These servants of Tzeentch are so imbued with transmogrifying magics that those in their proximity can be torn apart by these energies only to be remade in the form of a Tzaangor.

ORGANISATION

An Alter-kin Coven consists of the following units:

- 1 unit of Kairic Acolytes
- 1 unit of Tzaangors
- 1 unit of Tzaangor Skyfires

ABILITIES

Boon of Mutation: In each of your hero phases, roll a dice for each enemy unit that is within 3" of a unit from an Alter-kin Coven. On a roll of a 6, the unit being rolled for suffers D3 mortal wounds. If any models are slain in this manner, they are blessed with mutation and transmogrified into a Tzaangor. If there is already a friendly Tzaangor unit within 6" of the slain model's unit, add the Tzaangor to that unit, otherwise set it up as a new unit within 6" of the slain model's unit.

TZEENTCH
WITCHFYRE COVEN

Protected by a bodyguard of formidable Tzaangor Enlightened, the Kairic Acolytes of the Witchfyre Covens are true disciples of the wyrdflame. Many a foe has suffered blazing annihilation at the hands of its sorcerous brethren, incinerated by wave after wave of arcane fireballs.

ORGANISATION

A Witchfyre Coven consists of the following units:

- 2 units of Kairic Acolytes
- 1 unit of Tzaangor Enlightened

ABILITIES

Mastery of Wyrdflame: The Kairic Acolytes that form a Witchfyre Coven are the cult's most skilled at conjuring the flames of change, able to assail their foes with a relentless bombardment of eldritch fire. You can make a Sorcerous Bolt attack with each Kairic Acolyte model from a Witchfyre Coven in each of your hero phases.

TZEENTCH

SKYSHOAL COVEN

Leaving behind shimmering contrails, Skyshoal Covens whisk through the air with dazzling speed. The elite Tzaangors sweep over the heads of their prey upon Discs of Tzeentch, severing limbs and heads with the razor-edged protrusions of their daemonic mounts.

ORGANISATION

A Skyshoal Coven consists of the following units:

- 1 unit of Tzaangor Enlightened (must be mounted on Discs of Tzeentch)
- 2 units of Tzaangor Skyfires

ABILITIES

Scintillating Attack Run: The Tzaangor Enlightened and Skyfires of the Skyshoal Covens have learned to utilise the blade-like protrusions of their daemonic mounts to lethal effect. In each of your hero phases, you can move any units from a Skyshoal Coven up to 9" as if it were the movement phase (they cannot run as part of this move, and it does not stop them from moving normally later in the turn). After a unit moves in this manner, you can pick an enemy unit that it moved across. Roll a dice for each model in the Skyshoal Coven unit; for each roll of 6, the unit it moved across suffers a mortal wound.

TZEENTCH
TZAANGOR COVEN

In battle the sects of a Tzaangor Coven flock towards one another, drawing a rabid ferocity from each other's presence. Driven by ambition and the proximity of their savage kin, the Tzaangors attack in a flurry of blades and stabbing beaks, seeking to bring down their foe and gain Tzeentch's favour.

ORGANISATION

A Tzaangor Coven consists of the following units:

- 1 unit of Tzaangors
- 1 unit of Tzaangor Enlightened
- 1 unit of Tzaangor Skyfires

ABILITIES

Aspirant Gor-kin: If the unit of Tzaangors from a Tzaangor Coven is within 9" of the battalion's unit of Tzaangor Enlightened or Tzaangor Skyfires at the start of your hero phase, they may pile in and attack as if it were the combat phase. If the unit of Tzaangors is within 9" of both of these units at the start of your hero phase, then you can also add 1 to their wound rolls when they attack in this manner.

Ferocious Fighters: Vicious Beak attacks made by models from a Tzaangor Coven wound on a roll of 4+ instead of 5+.

TZEENTCH
CULT OF THE TRANSIENT FORM

None embrace the power of change as zealously as the Cult of the Transient Form. Many of its human members actively seek to be transformed into Tzaangors, whom they regard as closer to the Great Mutator in form and spirit, and the prideful Gor-kin are only too happy to indulge them. Death is seen not as the end for these fanatics, but as the gateway to a glorious new beginning. Enemies are horrified as the corpses of slain cultists quiver and spasm, their flesh running like candle wax, before rising once more as shrieking Tzaangors – or something altogether more terrifying…

ORGANISATION

The Cult of the Transient Form must contain the following:

- 1 Arcanite Cabal
- 1 Alter-kin Coven (the unit of Tzaangors must contain at least 20 models)

The Cult of the Transient Form may also contain:
- 0-8 warscroll battalions chosen in any combination from the following list:
  - Alter-kin Coven
  - Skyshoal Coven
  - Tzaangor Coven
  - Witchfyre Coven
- Any number of additional TZEENTCH ARCANITE units

If the Cult of the Transient Form contains at least 3 Covens, it gains the Destiny Preordained and Strength in Conviction abilities (pg 104).

ABILITIES

The Change-gift: Roll a dice each time a Kairic Acolyte from the Cult of the Transient Form is slain. On a roll of 6, they are blessed with new life and are transmogrified into a Tzaangor. If there is already a friendly Tzaangor unit within 6" of the slain model's unit, add the Tzaangor to that unit, otherwise set it up as a new unit within 6" of the slain model's unit. In addition, roll a dice each time a HERO from the Cult of the Transient Form is slain. On a roll of 6 they are reborn as a horrific Chaos Spawn; set up a Chaos Spawn under your control anywhere within 6" of the slain HERO model just before removing it.

TZEENTCH
THE PYROFANE CULT

The Pyrofane Cult and their splinter cults revel in destruction. Their arcane pyrotechnics build upon themselves, gathering strength like an out-of-control wildfire. Each burning bolt that they chant into existence sears with unnatural fury. Few dare stand before such an inferno for long, as the air itself begins to smoulder and smoke. Tzeentch blesses those who bring the corrupting flames to his enemies, granting the Pyrofane Cult's sorcerers the ability to cast flickering chainfires that leap from foe to foe. True glory comes only through fiery ruination.

ORGANISATION

The Pyrofane Cult must contain the following:

- 1 Arcanite Cabal
- 1 Witchfyre Coven (each unit of Kairic Acolytes must contain at least 20 models)

The Pyrofane Cult may also contain:
- 0-8 warscroll battalions chosen in any combination from the following list:
  - Alter-kin Coven
  - Skyshoal Coven
  - Tzaangor Coven
  - Witchfyre Coven
- Any number of additional TZEENTCH ARCANITE units

If the Pyrofane Cult contains at least 3 Covens, it gains the Destiny Preordained and Strength in Conviction abilities (pg 104).

ABILITIES

Arch-Pyromancers: You can add 1 to the wound rolls of Sorcerous Bolt attacks made by Kairic Acolytes from the Pyrofane Cult for each other unit from the battalion that attacked the target unit with Sorcerous Bolts earlier in the same phase. For example, if two units of Kairic Acolytes from the Pyrofane Cult had already targeted a unit with Sorcerous Bolts, you could add 2 to the wound rolls of the third unit that did so.

MAGIC

WIZARDS in the Pyrofane Cult know the following spell in addition to any others they know:

FLICKERING FIRES OF TZEENTCH
Flickering Fires of Tzeentch has a casting value of 7. If successfully cast, pick a visible enemy unit within 18" of the caster. That unit suffers D3 mortal wounds. In addition, roll a dice for each enemy unit within 3" of the unit you picked; on a roll of 4 or more, the unit being rolled for also suffers D3 mortal wounds.

WARSCROLLS

The warriors and creatures that battle in the Mortal Realms are incredibly diverse, each one fighting with their own unique weapons and combat abilities. To represent this, every model has a warscroll that lists the characteristics, weapons and abilities that apply to the model.

Every Citadel Miniature in the Warhammer range has its own warscroll, which provides you with all of the information needed to use that model in a game of *Warhammer Age of Sigmar*. This means that you can use any Citadel Miniatures in your collection as part of an army as long as you have the right warscrolls.

When fighting a battle, simply refer to the warscrolls for the models you are using. Warscrolls for all of the other models in the *Warhammer Age of Sigmar* range are available from Games Workshop. Just visit our website at games-workshop.com for more information on how to obtain them.

The key below explains what you will find on a warscroll, and the *Warhammer Age of Sigmar* rules sheet explains how this information is used in a game. The warscroll also includes a short piece of text explaining the background for the models and how they fight.

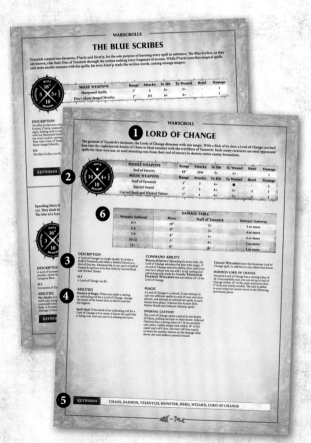

1. **Title:** The name of the model that the warscroll describes.

2. **Characteristics:** This set of characteristics tells you how fast, powerful and brave the model is, and how effective its weapons are.

3. **Description:** The description tells you what weapons the model can be armed with, and what upgrades (if any) it can be given. The description will also tell you if the model is fielded on its own as a single model, or as part of a unit. If the model is fielded as part of a unit, then the description will say how many models the unit should have (if you don't have enough models to field a unit, you can still field one unit with as many models as you have available).

4. **Abilities:** Abilities are things that the model can do during a game that are not covered by the standard game rules.

5. **Keywords:** All models have a list of keywords. Sometimes a rule will say that it only applies to models that have a specific keyword.

6. **Damage Table:** Some models have a damage table that is used to determine one or more of the model's characteristics. Look up the number of wounds the model has suffered to find the value of the characteristic in question.

HINTS & TIPS

Modifiers: Many warscrolls include modifiers that can affect characteristics. For example, a rule might add 1 to the Move characteristic of a model, or subtract 1 from the result of a hit roll. Modifiers are cumulative.

Random Values: Sometimes, the Move or weapon characteristics on a warscroll will have random values. For example, the Move characteristic for a model might be 2D6 (two dice rolls added together), whereas the Attacks characteristic of a weapon might be D6.

When a unit with a random Move characteristic is selected to move in the movement phase, roll the indicated number of dice. The total of the dice rolled is the Move characteristic for all models in the unit for the duration of that movement phase.

Generate any random values for a weapon (except Damage) each time it is chosen as the weapon for an attack.

Roll once and apply the result to all such weapons being used in the attack. The result applies for the rest of that phase. For Damage, generate a value for each weapon that inflicts damage.

When to Use Abilities: Abilities that are used at the start of a phase must be carried out before any other actions. By the same token, abilities used at the end of the phase are carried out after all normal activities for the phase are complete.

If you can use several abilities at the same time, you can decide in which order they are used. If both players can carry out abilities at the same time, the player whose turn is taking place uses their abilities first.

Save of '-': Some models have a Save of '-'. This means that they automatically fail all save rolls (do not make the roll, even if modifiers apply).

Keywords: Keywords are sometimes linked to (or tagged) by a rule. For example, a rule might say that it applies to 'all TZEENTCH models'. This means that it would apply to models that have the Tzeentch keyword on their warscroll.

Keywords can also be a useful way to decide which models to include in an army. For example, if you want to field a Tzeentch army, just use models that have the Tzeentch keyword.

Minimum Range: Some weapons have a minimum range. For example 6"-48". The weapon cannot shoot at an enemy unit that is within the minimum range.

Weapons: Some models can be armed with two identical weapons. When the model attacks with these weapons, do not double the number of attacks that the weapons make; usually, the model gets an additional ability instead.

LORD OF CHANGE

The greatest of Tzeentch's daemons, the Lords of Change shimmer with raw magic. With a flick of its claw, a Lord of Change can hurl foes into the nightmarish Realm of Chaos or blast enemies with the wyrdfires of Tzeentch. Such canny creatures can steal opponents' spells for their own use, or send mutating rays from their rod of sorcery to destroy entire enemy formations.

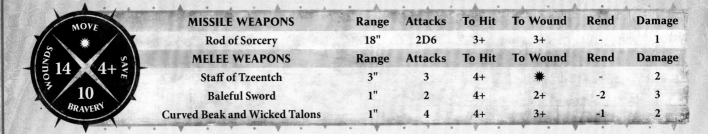

MISSILE WEAPONS	Range	Attacks	To Hit	To Wound	Rend	Damage
Rod of Sorcery	18"	2D6	3+	3+	-	1
MELEE WEAPONS	Range	Attacks	To Hit	To Wound	Rend	Damage
Staff of Tzeentch	3"	3	4+	✸	-	2
Baleful Sword	1"	2	4+	2+	-2	3
Curved Beak and Wicked Talons	1"	4	4+	3+	-1	2

Stats: WOUNDS 14, SAVE 4+, BRAVERY 10

DAMAGE TABLE			
Wounds Suffered	Move	Staff of Tzeentch	Infernal Gateway
0-3	10"	2+	3 or more
4-6	9"	3+	4 or more
7-9	8"	3+	4 or more
10-12	7"	4+	5 or more
13+	6"	4+	5 or more

DESCRIPTION
A Lord of Change is a single model. It carries a Staff of Tzeentch and either a Baleful Sword or a Rod of Sorcery. Alternatively, it can carry a Staff of Tzeentch and tear at its foes with its Curved Beak and Wicked Talons.

FLY
A Lord of Change can fly.

ABILITIES
Mastery of Magic: When you make a casting or unbinding roll for a Lord of Change, change the result of the lowest dice so that it matches the highest.

Spell-thief: If the result of an unbinding roll for a Lord of Change is 9 or more, it learns the spell that is being cast, and can cast it in subsequent turns.

COMMAND ABILITY
Beacon of Sorcery: Spreading its arms wide, the Lord of Change saturates the area with magic. If a Lord of Change uses this ability, then until your next hero phase you can add 1 to all casting and unbinding rolls made for friendly **TZEENTCH DAEMON WIZARDS** that are within 18" of the Lord of Change.

MAGIC
A Lord of Change is a wizard. It can attempt to cast two different spells in each of your own hero phases, and attempt to unbind two spells in each enemy hero phase. It knows the Arcane Bolt, Mystic Shield and Infernal Gateway spells.

INFERNAL GATEWAY
The Lord of Change opens a portal to the Realm of Chaos, pulling warriors to their doom. Infernal Gateway has a casting value of 7. If successfully cast, pick a visible enemy unit within 18" of the caster and roll 9 dice. For each roll that equals or beats the number shown on the damage table above, the unit suffers a mortal wound.

CHAOS WIZARDS know the Summon Lord of Change spell, in addition to any others they know.

SUMMON LORD OF CHANGE
Summon Lord of Change has a casting value of 10. If successfully cast, you can set up a Lord of Change within 18" of the caster and more than 9" from any enemy models. The unit is added to your army but cannot move in the following movement phase.

KAIROS FATEWEAVER

Kairos Fateweaver can see the past and the future, and uses this ability to twist destiny to suit his own malevolent purposes. The twin-headed terror is a master of magic, able to transform foes into tentacle-ridden Chaos Spawn or incinerate them with multicoloured blasts of fire. He is the Oracle of Tzeentch, and wherever he goes, change is sure to follow.

MOVE
WOUNDS 14 **SAVE** 4+
10
BRAVERY

MELEE WEAPONS	Range	Attacks	To Hit	To Wound	Rend	Damage
Staff of Tomorrow	3"	2	4+	✹	-1	2
Beaks and Claws	1"	5	4+	3+	-1	2

DAMAGE TABLE			
Wounds Suffered	Move	Staff of Tomorrow	Gift of Change
0-3	10"	2+	D6 mortal wounds
4-6	9"	3+	D6 mortal wounds
7-9	8"	3+	D3 mortal wounds
10-12	7"	4+	D3 mortal wounds
13+	6"	4+	1 mortal wound

DESCRIPTION
Kairos Fateweaver is a single model. He carries the arcane Staff of Tomorrow, and can tear at his foes with his sharp Beaks and Claws.

FLY
Kairos Fateweaver can fly.

ABILITIES
Mastery of Magic: When you make a casting or unbinding roll for Kairos Fateweaver, change the result of the lowest dice so that it matches the highest.

Oracle of Eternity: Once per battle, you can change the result of a single dice roll to the result of your choosing. However, this ability may not be used to affect the roll to see who takes the first turn in a battle round.

MAGIC
Kairos Fateweaver is a wizard. He can attempt to cast two different spells in each of your own hero phases and attempt to unbind two spells in each enemy hero phase. He knows the Arcane Bolt, Mystic Shield and Gift of Change spells. Kairos also knows the spells of all other **WIZARDS** from your army that are within 18" of him.

GIFT OF CHANGE
Kairos makes a burning sigil in the air and gifts his foes with the boon of mutating flesh. Gift of Change has a casting value of 8. If successfully cast, pick a visible enemy unit within 18" of the caster. That unit suffers a number of mortal wounds as shown in the damage table above. If any models were slain by this spell, you can set up a Chaos Spawn under your control within 3" of that unit.

KEYWORDS	CHAOS, DAEMON, TZEENTCH, MONSTER, HERO, WIZARD, LORD OF CHANGE, KAIROS FATEWEAVER

HERALD OF TZEENTCH
ON BURNING CHARIOT

Trailing flames and maniacal laughter, a Herald of Tzeentch streaks across the skies bringing with it fiery doom. While the Herald conjures firestorms to engulf the foe, the living chariot it rides seeks to sear all those in its path. Any who manage to close upon the speeding chariot must face the gnashing fangs of the Screamers bound to it, and strikes from the Herald's mutagenic staff of change.

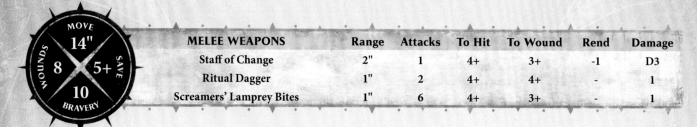

MELEE WEAPONS	Range	Attacks	To Hit	To Wound	Rend	Damage
Staff of Change	2"	1	4+	3+	-1	D3
Ritual Dagger	1"	2	4+	4+	-	1
Screamers' Lamprey Bites	1"	6	4+	3+	-	1

MOVE 14"
WOUNDS 8
SAVE 5+
BRAVERY 10

DESCRIPTION

A Herald of Tzeentch on Burning Chariot is a single model. The Screamers pulling the chariot attack with their vicious Lamprey Bites, while the Herald of Tzeentch strikes out with a Staff of Change or Ritual Dagger, and reads aloud from an Arcane Tome.

FLY

A Herald of Tzeentch on Burning Chariot can fly.

ABILITIES

Arcane Tome: Once per battle, the Herald can read from its Arcane Tome before attempting to cast a spell. You can roll three dice instead of two for that casting attempt.

Sky-sharks: Screamers that manage to latch their teeth into a larger creature will not let go easily, eventually tearing out huge chunks of bloodied flesh. The Screamers' Lamprey Bites attack inflicts D3 Damage if the target is a **Monster**.

Wake of Fire: After a Burning Chariot of Tzeentch moves in the movement phase, you can pick an enemy unit that it moved across. Roll a dice; on a roll of 4 or more, the unit suffers D3 mortal wounds.

MAGIC

A Herald of Tzeentch on Burning Chariot is a wizard. It can attempt to cast one spell in each of your own hero phases, and attempt to unbind one spell in each enemy hero phase. It knows the Arcane Bolt, Mystic Shield and Tzeentch's Firestorm spells.

TZEENTCH'S FIRESTORM

Searing balls of scarlet flame begin to whip around the caster before spiralling outwards to engulf nearby enemies. Tzeentch's Firestorm has a casting value of 9. If successfully cast, roll a dice for each enemy unit within 9". If the result is 4 or more, that unit suffers D3 mortal wounds.

Chaos Wizards know the Summon Burning Herald spell, in addition to any others they know.

SUMMON BURNING HERALD

Summon Burning Herald has a casting value of 7. If successfully cast, you can set up a Herald of Tzeentch on Burning Chariot within 18" of the caster and more than 9" from any enemy models. The unit is added to your army but cannot move in the following movement phase.

KEYWORDS	CHAOS, DAEMON, HORROR, TZEENTCH, HERO, WIZARD, HERALD ON BURNING CHARIOT

HERALD OF TZEENTCH

ON DISC

There is nowhere on the battlefield safe from a Herald riding a Disc of Tzeentch. Bolting through the air, the Herald conjures blue flames to hurl upon the foe before gliding out of reach. Should an enemy appear vulnerable, the Herald will dash in using its staff of change to deliver mutation-causing strikes, while the razor-sharp horns and teeth of the Disc deliver their own punishments.

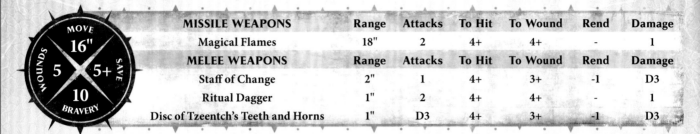

MISSILE WEAPONS	Range	Attacks	To Hit	To Wound	Rend	Damage
Magical Flames	18"	2	4+	4+	-	1
MELEE WEAPONS	**Range**	**Attacks**	**To Hit**	**To Wound**	**Rend**	**Damage**
Staff of Change	2"	1	4+	3+	-1	D3
Ritual Dagger	1"	2	4+	4+	-	1
Disc of Tzeentch's Teeth and Horns	1"	D3	4+	3+	-1	D3

Move 16" / Wounds 5 / Save 5+ / Bravery 10

DESCRIPTION

A Herald of Tzeentch on Disc is a single model. The Herald wields a Staff of Change or a Ritual Dagger, and carries an Arcane Tome. The Herald can also hurl Magical Flames at its foes, and its Disc can attack with its piercing Teeth and Horns.

FLY

A Herald of Tzeentch on Disc can fly.

ABILITIES

Arcane Tome: Once per battle, the Herald can read from its Arcane Tome before attempting to cast a spell. You can roll three dice instead of two for that casting attempt.

MAGIC

A Herald of Tzeentch on Disc is a wizard. It can attempt to cast one spell in each of your own hero phases, and attempt to unbind one spell in each enemy hero phase. It knows the Arcane Bolt, Mystic Shield and Blue Fire of Tzeentch spells.

BLUE FIRE OF TZEENTCH

Blue Fire of Tzeentch has a casting value of 4. If successfully cast, a tide of iridescent mutating flame surges forth. Pick a visible enemy unit within 18" of the caster. You roll 9 dice while your opponent rolls 1 die. The target unit suffers a mortal wound each time one of your dice matches the score rolled by your opponent.

CHAOS WIZARDS know the Summon Herald on Disc spell, in addition to any others they know.

SUMMON HERALD ON DISC

Summon Herald on Disc has a casting value of 5. If successfully cast, you can set up a Herald of Tzeentch on Disc within 18" of the caster and more than 9" from any enemy models. The unit is added to your army but cannot move in the following movement phase.

KEYWORDS | CHAOS, DAEMON, HORROR, TZEENTCH, HERO, WIZARD, HERALD ON DISC

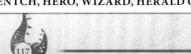

THE CHANGELING

None recognise the presence of the daemon known as the Changeling until it is already too late. A master of illusionary disguise, the Changeling secrets itself amongst its quarry, sowing confusion and misdirection amongst their ranks. Upon throwing aside its fleshly masquerade, the Changeling uses sorcery and its Trickster's Staff to openly blast its foes.

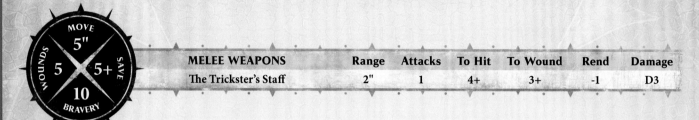

MELEE WEAPONS	Range	Attacks	To Hit	To Wound	Rend	Damage
The Trickster's Staff	2"	1	4+	3+	-1	D3

DESCRIPTION
The Changeling is a single model. It is armed with the Trickster's Staff.

ABILITIES
Arch-deceiver: At the start of the battle, you can set up the Changeling in your opponent's territory as though it were part of their army. Enemy units treat it as part of their own army – they can move within 3" of it but they cannot target it with spells or attacks, and so on. If it attacks, casts or unbinds a spell, or is within 3" of an enemy **HERO** in your opponent's hero phase, it is revealed and this ability no longer has an effect.

Puckish Misdirection: Until the Changeling is revealed, you can pick one unit within 9" of it in each enemy hero phase. That unit halves its Move until your next hero phase.

Formless Horror: Instead of using the Trickster's Staff in the combat phase, you can pick a melee weapon wielded by the target unit and attack with that weapon, using its profile.

MAGIC
The Changeling is a wizard. It can cast one spell in each of your own hero phases, and attempt to unbind one spell in each enemy hero phase. It knows the Arcane Bolt and Mystic Shield spells. The Changeling also knows the spells of any **WIZARD** that is within 9" of it.

KEYWORDS	CHAOS, DAEMON, HORROR, TZEENTCH, HERO, WIZARD, THE CHANGELING

HERALD OF TZEENTCH

Wielding the pink changefire of its patron, a Herald of Tzeentch is a luminescent servant of the Changer of the Ways. By magic and manipulation of the strands of fate, the Herald seeks to execute its portion of Tzeentch's ineffable plans. Any that attempt to thwart its anarchic cause will soon feel the wrath of living flames or the mutating blows of its staff of change.

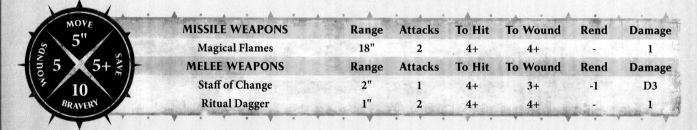

MISSILE WEAPONS	Range	Attacks	To Hit	To Wound	Rend	Damage
Magical Flames	18"	2	4+	4+	-	1
MELEE WEAPONS	**Range**	**Attacks**	**To Hit**	**To Wound**	**Rend**	**Damage**
Staff of Change	2"	1	4+	3+	-1	D3
Ritual Dagger	1"	2	4+	4+	-	1

DESCRIPTION
A Herald of Tzeentch is a single model. It is armed with a Staff of Change or a Ritual Dagger, and carries an Arcane Tome. It can also hurl Magical Flames at its foes.

ABILITIES
Arcane Tome: Once per battle, the Herald can read from its Arcane Tome before attempting to cast a spell. You can roll three dice instead of two for that casting attempt.

Fortune and Fate: If you roll a 9 or more for a Herald of Tzeentch's casting roll, it can attempt to cast one extra spell this hero phase (it must be a different spell).

MAGIC
A Herald of Tzeentch is a wizard. It can attempt to cast one spell in each of your own hero phases, and attempt to unbind one spell in each enemy hero phase. It knows the Arcane Bolt, Mystic Shield and Pink Fire of Tzeentch spells.

PINK FIRE OF TZEENTCH
Pink Fire of Tzeentch has a casting value of 9. If successfully cast, a tide of writhing warpflame engulfs the foe. Pick a visible enemy unit within 18" of the caster. That unit suffers D6 mortal wounds.

CHAOS WIZARDS know the Summon Herald of Tzeentch spell, in addition to any others they know.

SUMMON HERALD OF TZEENTCH
Summon Herald of Tzeentch has a casting value of 5. If successfully cast, you can set up a Herald of Tzeentch within 18" of the caster and more than 9" from any enemy models. The Herald is added to your army but cannot move in the following movement phase.

KEYWORDS	CHAOS, DAEMON, HORROR, TZEENTCH, HERO, WIZARD, HERALD OF TZEENTCH

THE BLUE SCRIBES

Tzeentch created two daemons, P'tarix and Xirat'p, for the sole purpose of learning every spell in existence. The Blue Scribes, as they are known, ride their Disc of Tzeentch through the realms seeking every fragment of arcana. While P'tarix inscribes magical spells and stabs nearby enemies with his quills, his twin Xirat'p reads the written words, casting strange magics.

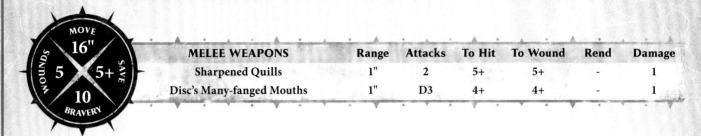

MELEE WEAPONS	Range	Attacks	To Hit	To Wound	Rend	Damage
Sharpened Quills	1"	2	5+	5+	-	1
Disc's Many-fanged Mouths	1"	D3	4+	4+	-	1

MOVE 16"
WOUNDS 5
SAVE 5+
BRAVERY 10

DESCRIPTION

The Blue Scribes are a single model. One of the Scribes, P'tarix, transcribes pages of magical sigils, halting only to stab at approaching enemies with his Sharpened Quills, while Xirat'p reads his twin's scrawl, casting spells hither and yon. They ride a Disc of Tzeentch which attacks with its Many-fanged Mouths.

FLY

The Blue Scribes can fly.

ABILITIES

Frantic Scribbling: Roll a dice each time a **WIZARD** within 18" of the Blue Scribes successfully casts a spell (whether or not it is unbound); on a 4 or more the Scribes learn that spell and can attempt to cast it in subsequent turns.

Scrolls of Sorcery: Once in each of your hero phases, the Blue Scribes can read from their Scrolls of Sorcery instead of making a casting attempt. If they do, roll a dice; on a 1, they can't decipher the scrawls and the casting attempt automatically fails, but on a 2 or more, that spell is successfully cast and can only be unbound on a roll of 9 or more.

MAGIC

The Blue Scribes can attempt to cast one spell in each of your own hero phases, and attempt to unbind one spell in each enemy hero phase. They know the Arcane Bolt, Mystic Shield and Boon of Tzeentch spells.

BOON OF TZEENTCH

The Blue Scribes reach forth, tapping into an unseen hoard of arcane power. Boon of Tzeentch has a casting value of 4. If successfully cast, you can re-roll failed casting rolls made for **TZEENTCH WIZARDS** within 18" of the Blue Scribes for the rest of the hero phase.

KEYWORDS | CHAOS, DAEMON, HORROR, TZEENTCH, HERO, WIZARD, THE BLUE SCRIBES

SCREAMERS OF TZEENTCH

Speeding blurs that leave shimmering trails of change-magics in the air behind them, Screamers streak across the skies with a wailing cry. They slash foes they pass with razor-sharp horns and fins, before darting down to savage their chosen quarry with gnashing teeth. The bite of a Screamer is fierce, their fang-filled maws able to gouge out large chunks of flesh.

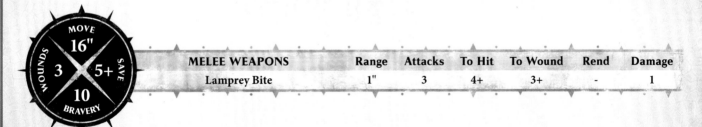

MELEE WEAPONS	Range	Attacks	To Hit	To Wound	Rend	Damage
Lamprey Bite	1"	3	4+	3+	-	1

MOVE 16"
WOUNDS 3
SAVE 5+
BRAVERY 10

DESCRIPTION

A unit of Screamers of Tzeentch has 3 or more models, which tear into their prey with their Lamprey Bites.

FLY

Screamers of Tzeentch can fly.

ABILITIES

Sky-sharks: Screamers that manage to latch their teeth into a larger creature will not let go easily, eventually tearing out huge chunks of bloodied flesh. A Screamer's Lamprey Bite attack inflicts D3 Damage if the target is a **MONSTER**.

Slashing Fins: After a unit of Screamers moves in the movement phase, you can pick an enemy unit that it moved across. Roll a dice for each Screamer that passed across it; for each roll of 6, that unit suffers a mortal wound.

Locus of Change: Whilst this unit is within 9" of any **TZEENTCH DAEMON HEROES** from your army, they are surrounded by a twisting aura of change; if an enemy model targets such a unit, your opponent must treat any hit rolls of 6 as hit rolls of 1 instead.

MAGIC

CHAOS WIZARDS know the Summon Screamers spell, in addition to any others they know.

SUMMON SCREAMERS

Summon Screamers has a casting value of 6. If successfully cast, you can set up a unit of up to 3 Screamers of Tzeentch within 18" of the caster and more than 9" from any enemy models. The unit is added to your army but cannot move in the following movement phase. If the result of the casting roll was 11 or more, set up a unit of up to 6 Screamers of Tzeentch instead.

KEYWORDS | CHAOS, DAEMON, TZEENTCH, SCREAMERS

BURNING CHARIOTS OF TZEENTCH

Pulled through the skies by a pair of Screamers, a Burning Chariot of Tzeentch rides upon a wave of multicoloured flames that scorch all in their wake. The Exalted Flamer that writhes and twists upon the back of the chariot vomits sheets of billowing fire – an unnatural conflagration that even when put out will rage up once more, burning foes again and again.

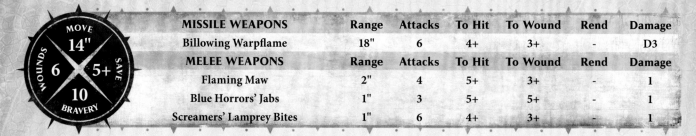

MISSILE WEAPONS	Range	Attacks	To Hit	To Wound	Rend	Damage
Billowing Warpflame	18"	6	4+	3+	-	D3
MELEE WEAPONS	Range	Attacks	To Hit	To Wound	Rend	Damage
Flaming Maw	2"	4	5+	3+	-	1
Blue Horrors' Jabs	1"	3	5+	5+	-	1
Screamers' Lamprey Bites	1"	6	4+	3+	-	1

MOVE 14"
WOUNDS 6
SAVE 5+
BRAVERY 10

DESCRIPTION
A unit of Burning Chariots of Tzeentch can have any number of models. An Exalted Flamer stands atop each, spouting Billowing Warpflame as it careens past the enemy, or stopping to savage them with its Flaming Maw. Each Flamer is attended to by a trio of grumpy Blue Horrors, who jab at foes who are close enough. Each chariot is pulled by a pair of Screamers of Tzeentch that attack with their Lamprey Bites.

FLY
A Burning Chariot of Tzeentch can fly.

ABILITIES
Capricious Warpflame: Roll a dice at the end of the shooting phase for each unit that suffered wounds from this model's Billowing Warpflame. On a 4 or more, that unit suffers an additional D3 mortal wounds as the mutating flames refuse to die. On a 1, Tzeentch's fickle nature reveals itself and one model in that unit heals D3 wounds instead.

Sky-sharks: Screamers that manage to latch their teeth into a larger creature will not let go easily, eventually tearing out huge chunks of bloodied flesh. The Screamers' Lamprey Bites attack inflicts D3 Damage if the target is a **MONSTER**.

Wake of Fire: After a Burning Chariot moves in the movement phase, you can pick an enemy unit that it moved across. Roll a dice; on a roll of 4 or more, the unit suffers D3 mortal wounds.

MAGIC
CHAOS WIZARDS know the Summon Burning Chariot spell, in addition to any others they know.

SUMMON BURNING CHARIOT
Summon Burning Chariot has a casting value of 8. If successfully cast, you can set up a Burning Chariot of Tzeentch within 18" of the caster and more than 9" from any enemy models. This model is added to your army but cannot move in the following movement phase.

KEYWORDS CHAOS, DAEMON, FLAMER, HORROR, TZEENTCH, BURNING CHARIOTS

EXALTED FLAMERS OF TZEENTCH

An Exalted Flamer of Tzeentch can project gouts of multicoloured flame, turning entire enemy units into piles of blackened bones. The shifting warpflames seem to have a mind of their own, forming hideous faces and ominous sigils with their crackling tongues of fire. Should any foes get through the raging inferno, the Exalted Flamer will savage them with its flame-wreathed maw.

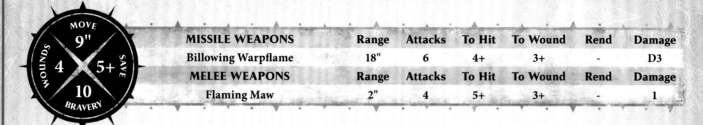

MISSILE WEAPONS	Range	Attacks	To Hit	To Wound	Rend	Damage
Billowing Warpflame	18"	6	4+	3+	-	D3
MELEE WEAPONS	Range	Attacks	To Hit	To Wound	Rend	Damage
Flaming Maw	2"	4	5+	3+	-	1

MOVE 9" / WOUNDS 4 / SAVE 5+ / BRAVERY 10

DESCRIPTION
A unit of Exalted Flamers of Tzeentch can have any number of models. An Exalted Flamer spouts Billowing Warpflame as it floats past the enemy, or leaps to savage them with its Flaming Maw.

FLY
Exalted Flamers propel themselves across the battlefield in great leaps and bounds. Exalted Flamers of Tzeentch can fly.

ABILITIES
Capricious Warpflame: Roll a dice at the end of the shooting phase for each unit that suffered wounds from this model's Billowing Warpflame. On a 4 or more, that unit suffers an additional D3 mortal wounds as the mutating flames refuse to die. On a 1, Tzeentch's fickle nature reveals itself and one model in that unit heals D3 wounds instead.

MAGIC
CHAOS WIZARDS know the Summon Exalted Flamer spell, in addition to any others they know.

SUMMON EXALTED FLAMER
Summon Exalted Flamer has a casting value of 6. If successfully cast, you can set up an Exalted Flamer of Tzeentch within 18" of the caster and more than 9" from any enemy models. This model is added to your army but cannot move in the following movement phase. If the casting roll was 11 or more, you can set up a unit of up to 3 Exalted Flamers instead.

KEYWORDS | CHAOS, DAEMON, FLAMER, TZEENTCH, EXALTED FLAMERS

FLAMERS OF TZEENTCH

Bounding in a disturbing fashion, Flamers of Tzeentch spring towards the foe spouting wyrdflame, the warpfires of Chaos itself. The supernatural flames writhe and leer, but most of all they burn, scorching the foe's flesh, bones and soul. Yet the Changer of the Ways is fickle, and fires that have burnt out may leap to life again, or even heal the afflicted.

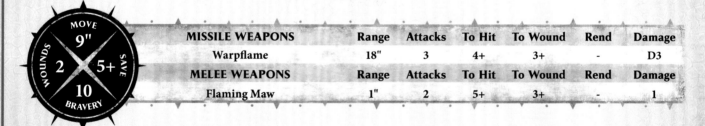

MISSILE WEAPONS	Range	Attacks	To Hit	To Wound	Rend	Damage
Warpflame	18"	3	4+	3+	-	D3
MELEE WEAPONS	Range	Attacks	To Hit	To Wound	Rend	Damage
Flaming Maw	1"	2	5+	3+	-	1

MOVE 9" / WOUNDS 2 / SAVE 5+ / BRAVERY 10

DESCRIPTION
A unit of Flamers of Tzeentch has 3 or more models. They spout searing gouts of Warpflame from their many mouths and gnash at their foes with Flaming Maws.

FLY
Flamers of Tzeentch propel themselves forwards in great leaps and bounds. Flamers can fly.

PYROCASTER
The leader of this unit is the Pyrocaster. A Pyrocaster makes 4 attacks with its Warpflame instead of 3.

ABILITIES
Capricious Warpflame: Roll a dice at the end of the shooting phase for each unit that suffered wounds from a Flamer's Warpflame. On a 4 or more, that unit suffers an additional D3 mortal wounds as the mutating flames refuse to die. On a 1, Tzeentch's fickle nature reveals itself and one model in that unit heals D3 wounds instead.

Locus of Transmogrification: Roll a dice each time a model in this unit is slain within 9" of a **TZEENTCH DAEMON HERO** from your army; on a 6, add two Flamer models to this unit.

MAGIC
CHAOS WIZARDS know the Summon Flamers of Tzeentch spell, in addition to any others they know.

SUMMON FLAMERS OF TZEENTCH
Summon Flamers of Tzeentch has a casting value of 6. If successfully cast, you can set up a unit of up to 3 Flamers of Tzeentch within 18" of the caster and more than 9" from any enemy models. The unit is added to your army but cannot move in the following movement phase. If the result of the casting roll was 11 or more, set up a unit of up to 6 Flamers of Tzeentch instead.

KEYWORDS | CHAOS, DAEMON, TZEENTCH, FLAMERS

PINK HORRORS OF TZEENTCH

Gibbering nonsense with lunatic energy, the luminescent Pink Horrors whirl and flail their arms, generating raw magic that fills the air. En masse, the Pink Horrors give rise to so much arcane force that they can hurl blasts of unnatural fire at the enemy. In combat the Pink Horrors use their powerful hands to choke, and should they be slain, they split in twain to form two Blue Horrors.

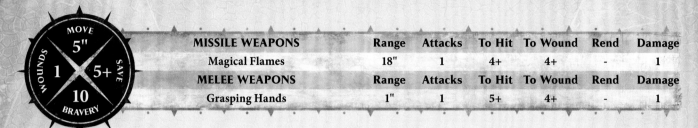

MOVE 5"
WOUNDS 1
SAVE 5+
BRAVERY 10

MISSILE WEAPONS	Range	Attacks	To Hit	To Wound	Rend	Damage
Magical Flames	18"	1	4+	4+	-	1
MELEE WEAPONS	Range	Attacks	To Hit	To Wound	Rend	Damage
Grasping Hands	1"	1	5+	4+	-	1

DESCRIPTION
A unit of Pink Horrors of Tzeentch has 10 or more models. They hurl Magical Flames at their enemies, and strangle them with their Grasping Hands.

IRIDESCENT HORROR
The leader of this unit is the Iridescent Horror. An Iridescent Horror makes 2 attacks rather than 1 with its Grasping Hands.

ICON BEARER
Models in this unit may be Icon Bearers. If you roll a 1 when taking a battleshock test for a unit that includes any Icon Bearers, reality blinks and the daemonic horde is bolstered. Add D6 Pink Horrors to the unit.

HORNBLOWER
Models in this unit can be Hornblowers. Your opponent must re-roll battleshock tests of 1 for units that are within 6" of any Hornblowers.

ABILITIES
Flickering Flames: You can add 1 to hit rolls made for a Pink Horror's Magical Flames attack if its unit contains 20 or more models.

Locus of Conjuration: You can add 1 to any casting rolls made for this unit if it is within 9" of any **Tzeentch Daemon Heroes** from your army.

MAGIC
A unit of Pink Horrors can attempt to cast one spell in each of your own hero phases, and attempt to unbind one spell in each enemy hero phase. Pink Horrors know the Arcane Bolt and Mystic Shield spells.

Chaos Wizards know the Summon Pink Horrors spell, in addition to any others they know.

SUMMON PINK HORRORS
Summon Pink Horrors has a casting value of 6. If successfully cast, you can set up a unit of up to 10 Pink Horrors within 18" of the caster and more than 9" from any enemy models. The unit is added to your army but cannot move in the following movement phase. If the result of the casting roll was 11 or more, set up a unit of up to 20 Pink Horrors instead.

KEYWORDS	CHAOS, DAEMON, TZEENTCH, WIZARD, PINK HORRORS

BLUE HORRORS OF TZEENTCH

Casting vindictive glares at their enemies and blasting them with mystical fire, Blue Horrors are as resentful and bitter as their pink cousins are gleeful and capricious. Muttering glumly, Blue Horrors cast azure flames from their fingertips, stomping and protesting as they do so. Should a Blue Horror be slain, it groans and flashes into glaring flames as a pair of Brimstone Horrors replaces it.

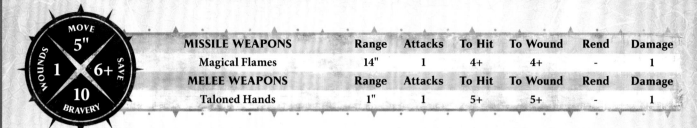

MISSILE WEAPONS	Range	Attacks	To Hit	To Wound	Rend	Damage
Magical Flames	14"	1	4+	4+	-	1
MELEE WEAPONS	Range	Attacks	To Hit	To Wound	Rend	Damage
Taloned Hands	1"	1	5+	5+	-	1

MOVE 5"
WOUNDS 1
SAVE 6+
BRAVERY 10

DESCRIPTION
A unit of Blue Horrors of Tzeentch has 10 or more models. They hurl Magical Flames at their enemies or slash at them with their Taloned Hands.

ABILITIES
Split: If a friendly unit of Pink Horrors suffers any casualties during a hero, shooting or combat phase, the slain Horrors will split and create Blue Horrors at the end of that phase (after all other units have performed their actions and made their attacks). Two Blue Horrors are created for each slain Pink Horror – if there is already a friendly Blue Horror unit within 6" of the Pink Horrors, add the Blue Horrors to that unit, otherwise set them up as a new unit within 6" of the unit of Pink Horrors.

If a rule causes a whole unit of Pink Horrors to be removed at once (excluding battleshock), you can immediately create a unit of Blue Horrors, just before removing the last model from the Pink Horrors unit. The unit of Blue Horrors has two models for each model in the unit of Pink Horrors at the point at which it is removed, and must be set up with all models within 6" of the last model from the Pink Horrors unit.

KEYWORDS	CHAOS, DAEMON, TZEENTCH, BLUE HORRORS

BRIMSTONE HORRORS OF TZEENTCH

When a Blue Horror is wounded it vanishes in a cloud of smoke and blue flame, replaced with a pair of Brimstone Horrors. Savage little sprites formed from living fire, these diminutive daemons leap and crackle as they worry at their enemies' shins and set fire to their battle-garb, eager to wreak as much flaming damage as their mite-sized forms allow.

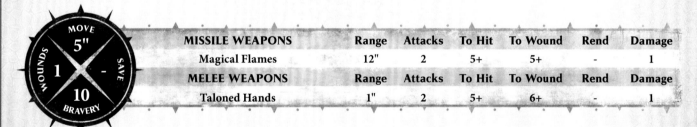

MISSILE WEAPONS	Range	Attacks	To Hit	To Wound	Rend	Damage
Magical Flames	12"	2	5+	5+	-	1
MELEE WEAPONS	Range	Attacks	To Hit	To Wound	Rend	Damage
Taloned Hands	1"	2	5+	6+	-	1

MOVE 5"
WOUNDS 1
SAVE -
BRAVERY 10

DESCRIPTION
A unit of Brimstone Horrors of Tzeentch has 10 or more models – each model consists of a pair of Brimstone Horrors. They hurl Magical Flames at their enemies or grab at them with their Taloned Hands.

ABILITIES
Split Again: If a friendly unit of Blue Horrors suffers any casualties during a hero, shooting or combat phase, the slain Horrors will split and create Brimstone Horrors at the end of that phase (after all other units have performed their actions and made their attacks). One model (remember that each model represents a pair of Brimstone Horrors) is created for each slain Blue Horror – if there is already a friendly Brimstone Horror unit within 6" of the Blue Horrors, add the Brimstone Horrors to that unit, otherwise set them up as a new unit within 6" of the unit of Blue Horrors.

If a rule causes a whole unit of Blue Horrors to be removed at once (excluding battleshock), you can immediately create a unit of Brimstone Horrors, just before removing the last model from the Blue Horrors unit. The unit of Brimstone Horrors has one model for each model in the unit of Blue Horrors at the point at which it is removed, and must be set up with all models within 6" of the last model from the Blue Horrors unit.

KEYWORDS	CHAOS, DAEMON, TZEENTCH, BRIMSTONE HORRORS

TZAANGOR SHAMAN

Mounted atop a Disc of Tzeentch, a Tzaangor Shaman is an agent of change in Tzeentch's service. With dark magics the Shaman will grant a boon of mutation to his foes, transforming them as they writhe and scream into a more pleasing form – that of a Tzaangor. No weakling in combat, the Tzaangor Shaman is a savage fighter, with horns and claws and a formidable staff of change.

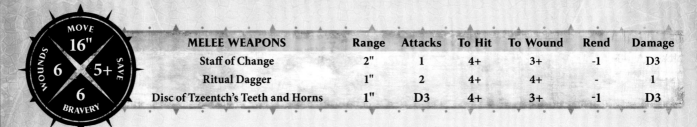

MELEE WEAPONS	Range	Attacks	To Hit	To Wound	Rend	Damage
Staff of Change	2"	1	4+	3+	-1	D3
Ritual Dagger	1"	2	4+	4+	-	1
Disc of Tzeentch's Teeth and Horns	1"	D3	4+	3+	-1	D3

MOVE 16"
WOUNDS 6
SAVE 5+
BRAVERY 6

DESCRIPTION

A Tzaangor Shaman is a single model. The Shaman wields a Staff of Change and a Ritual Dagger, and carries a Sorcerous Elixir. The Disc of Tzeentch that bears the Shaman to battle can attack with its piercing Teeth and Horns.

FLY

A Tzaangor Shaman can fly.

ABILITIES

Sorcerous Elixir: Once per battle, at the start of your hero phase, you can choose for a Tzaangor Shaman to drain the contents of its vial in order to augment its sorcerous might. On a turn in which you do so, you can attempt to cast a second spell with the Tzaangor Shaman (this can even be the same spell), and can choose to re-roll one or both of the dice when making your casting rolls.

MAGIC

A Tzaangor Shaman is a wizard. It can attempt to cast one spell in each of your own hero phases, and attempt to unbind one spell in each enemy hero phase. It knows the Arcane Bolt, Mystic Shield and Boon of Mutation spells.

BOON OF MUTATION

The Tzaangor Shaman curses its foes with the dubious gift of Tzeentch's mutagenic power, transforming its victims into a form altogether more pleasing. Boon of Mutation has a casting value of 7. If successfully cast, pick a visible enemy unit within 18" of the Tzaangor Shaman. The unit you pick suffers D3 mortal wounds. For each model that is slain by this spell, set up a new Tzaangor model – if there is already a friendly unit of Tzaangors within 6" of the unit you picked, add the Tzaangors to that unit, otherwise set them up as a new unit within 6" of the unit you picked.

KEYWORDS	CHAOS, GOR, DAEMON, TZEENTCH, ARCANITE, HERO, WIZARD, TZAANGOR SHAMAN

GAUNT SUMMONER OF TZEENTCH

There are but nine Gaunt Summoners, one of the most powerful orders of sorcerers dedicated to Tzeentch. Gazing into infinity with a myriad glistening eyes, a Gaunt Summoner calls forth daemons from the Realm of Chaos or summons sheets of infernal flames to engulf the foe. Those who dare approach too close are stabbed with a mutation-causing warptongue blade.

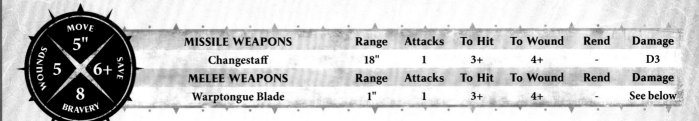

MISSILE WEAPONS	Range	Attacks	To Hit	To Wound	Rend	Damage
Changestaff	18"	1	3+	4+	-	D3
MELEE WEAPONS	Range	Attacks	To Hit	To Wound	Rend	Damage
Warptongue Blade	1"	1	3+	4+	-	See below

MOVE 5"
WOUNDS 5
SAVE 6+
BRAVERY 8

DESCRIPTION

A Gaunt Summoner of Tzeentch is a single model. He is armed with a Changestaff that can blast his enemies with the iridescent fires of Tzeentch, and a Warptongue Blade. He is never without a Book of Profane Secrets, with which he can call cohorts of daemons to the battlefield through a Realmgate.

ABILITIES

Book of Profane Secrets: If a Gaunt Summoner is within 9" of a **Realmgate** at the start of its movement phase, it can summon a unit of **Chaos Daemons** to the battlefield, adding it to your army. Place the unit so that all models are within 6" of the Realmgate and more than 9" away from any enemy units. This is the summoned unit's move for the movement phase.

Warptongue Blade: The body of anyone cut by a Warptongue Blade is wracked with sickening and uncontrollable mutations. If a Warptongue Blade inflicts damage on an enemy unit, roll two dice. If the roll is higher than the enemy unit's Bravery, one model in the unit is slain. Otherwise, the blade inflicts 1 wound.

MAGIC

A Gaunt Summoner of Tzeentch is a wizard. He can attempt to cast two different spells in each of your hero phases, and attempt to unbind two spells in each enemy hero phase. A Gaunt Summoner knows the Arcane Bolt, Mystic Shield and Infernal Flames spells.

INFERNAL FLAMES

The Gaunt Summoner conjures a rolling wave of scorching wyrdfire that engulfs enemy formations. Infernal Flames has a casting value of 8. If successfully cast, pick a visible enemy unit and roll 1 dice for each model in the target unit that is within 18" of the caster; the unit suffers 1 mortal wound for each roll of 4 or more. Roll 3 dice for each **Monster** or **War Machine** in the target unit, rather than only 1 dice.

KEYWORDS	CHAOS, DAEMON, MORTAL, TZEENTCH, ARCANITE, EVERCHOSEN, HERO, WIZARD, GAUNT SUMMONER

CURSELING, EYE OF TZEENTCH

Blessed with a Tretchlet – a daemon homunculus that can smell lies as they are spoken – a Curseling is an important leader of rituals in any Arcanite Cult. On the battlefield, Curselings are powerful fighters that can also steal enemy spells, reworking them in order to hurl them back at the foe.

MELEE WEAPONS	Range	Attacks	To Hit	To Wound	Rend	Damage
Blazing Sword	1"	3	3+	4+	-1	1
Threshing Flail	1"	3	4+	3+	-	1
Staff of Tzeentch	2"	1	5+	4+	-	D3

DESCRIPTION
A Curseling, Eye of Tzeentch, is a single model. He wields a Blazing Sword, a Threshing Flail and a Staff of Tzeentch.

ABILITIES
Vessel of Chaos: Each time a Curseling successfully unbinds an enemy spell, he can immediately attempt to cast it himself even though it is your opponent's hero phase. If this spell is cast, your opponent cannot attempt to unbind it.

MAGIC
A Curseling is a wizard. He can attempt to cast two different spells in each of your hero phases, and attempt to unbind two spells in each enemy hero phase. He knows the Arcane Bolt, Mystic Shield and Glean Magic spells.

GLEAN MAGIC
The Curseling reaches into his adversary's mind, and steals arcane knowledge to use for his own ends. Glean Magic has a casting value of 3. If successfully cast, pick an enemy **WIZARD** within 24", choose one of the spells from their warscroll and roll two dice. If the result is equal to or greater than the casting value of the chosen spell, the Curseling learns that spell and can use it for the rest of the battle.

KEYWORDS	CHAOS, MORTAL, TZEENTCH, ARCANITE, HERO, WIZARD, CURSELING

MAGISTER

Magisters are powerful sorcerers in service to Tzeentch. Filled with eldritch energies, a Magister can wield fantastical fires to scorch the foe, or transform an enemy into the squelching, misshapen form of a Chaos Spawn. As a member of the cabal of an Arcanite Cult, a Magister will use all his fell powers to inflict change and ruin upon the Mortal Realms in the name of the Great Conspirator.

MISSILE WEAPONS	Range	Attacks	To Hit	To Wound	Rend	Damage
Tzeentchian Runestaff	18"	1	3+	4+	-	D3
MELEE WEAPONS	**Range**	**Attacks**	**To Hit**	**To Wound**	**Rend**	**Damage**
Warpsteel Sword	1"	1	4+	4+	-	1

DESCRIPTION
A Magister is a single model. It is armed with a Warpsteel Sword, and looses bolts of flickering energy from its Tzeentchian Runestaff.

ABILITIES
Magic-touched: Magisters are attuned to magical energy like no other. If the result of a casting roll for this model is a double, whether or not the spell is successfully cast, it can attempt to cast another spell this turn.

MAGIC
A Magister is a wizard. It can attempt to cast one spell in each of your hero phases, and attempt to unbind one spell in each enemy hero phase. It knows the Arcane Bolt, Mystic Shield and Bolt of Change spells.

BOLT OF CHANGE
The Magister hurls a coruscating bolt of energy at the foe, causing their flesh to run like wax and remould into a form more pleasing to Tzeentch. Bolt of Change has a casting value of 7. If successfully cast, pick a visible enemy unit within 18" of the caster. That unit suffers D3 mortal wounds. Roll a dice for each model slain by Bolt of Change; if any of the results are a 4 or more, you can set up one Chaos Spawn under your control within 3" of the target unit.

KEYWORDS	CHAOS, MORTAL, TZEENTCH, ARCANITE, HERO, WIZARD, MAGISTER

FATEMASTER

More than just a powerful warrior, a Fatemaster is surrounded by an aura of change, a destiny-twisting zone that aids those mortals who follow the Great Schemer. Mounted atop a Disc of Tzeentch, a Fatemaster streaks into the midst of combat, slicing foes down with his fireglaive while manipulating fortune for the benefit of his Arcanite Cult.

MELEE WEAPONS	Range	Attacks	To Hit	To Wound	Rend	Damage
Fireglaive of Tzeentch	2"	3	3+	4+	-	D3
Disc of Tzeentch's Protruding Blades	1"	D3	4+	4+	-	1

MOVE 16" · **WOUNDS** 6 · **SAVE** 4+ · **BRAVERY** 8

DESCRIPTION
A Fatemaster is a single model. He wields a Fireglaive of Tzeentch, carries a Soulbound Shield, and rides a Disc of Tzeentch that assails the foe with its Protruding Blades.

FLY
A Fatemaster can fly.

ABILITIES
Soulbound Shield: If this model suffers any wounds or mortal wounds as the result of a spell, roll a dice. If the result is 4 or more, the wounds are ignored.

Hovering Disc of Tzeentch: Add 2 to the result of any save rolls for this model in the combat phase unless the attacker can fly.

COMMAND ABILITY
Lord of Fate: Tzeentch's chosen disciples can affect the destiny of those around them. If a Fatemaster uses this ability, roll a dice. Until your next hero phase, any time you make a dice roll for this model or a **TZEENTCH MORTAL** unit within 9", and the result matches that on the dice you rolled in the hero phase, you can choose to re-roll it.

KEYWORDS CHAOS, MORTAL, DAEMON, TZEENTCH, ARCANITE, HERO, FATEMASTER

OGROID THAUMATURGE

Combining bestial strength and ferocity with dark occult powers, the Ogroid Thaumaturge is a deadly foe. With snarled invocations the Thaumaturge hurls roiling blasts of fiery energy into the enemy ranks, before stampeding into the midst of its reeling foes to gore and pummel the survivors to bloody ruin. From the ashes of its flaming blasts step Horrors – daemons summoned from the beyond.

MELEE WEAPONS	Range	Attacks	To Hit	To Wound	Rend	Damage
Thaumaturge Staff	2"	2	3+	3+	-1	D3
Great Horns	1"	1	3+	3+	-2	3
Cloven Hooves	1"	4	4+	3+	-	1

MOVE 6" · **WOUNDS** 8 · **SAVE** 5+ · **BRAVERY** 8

DESCRIPTION
An Ogroid Thaumaturge is a single model. It smashes its foes with its Thaumaturge Staff, gores them with its Great Horns, and grinds them underfoot with its Cloven Hooves.

ABILITIES
Brutal Rage: If this model has suffered 5 or more wounds, add 1 to all of its hit rolls but subtract 1 from all of its casting and unbinding rolls (healing wounds may mean the Thaumaturge ceases to be enraged).

Mighty Bulk: After this model completes a charge move, pick an enemy unit within 1"; that unit suffers D3 mortal wounds.

Overwhelming Power: This model heals 1 wound in each of its hero phases.

MAGIC
An Ogroid Thaumaturge is a wizard. It can attempt to cast one spell in each of your own hero phases, and attempt to unbind one spell in each enemy hero phase. An Ogroid Thaumaturge knows the Arcane Bolt, Mystic Shield and Fireblast spells.

FIREBLAST
A Fireblast spell engulfs the target in coruscating flames from which capering daemons spring forth. Fireblast has a casting value of 7. If successfully cast, pick a visible enemy unit within 18" of the caster. The unit you pick suffers D6 mortal wounds. After the damage has been inflicted, you can set up a unit of Pink, Blue or Brimstone Horrors within 1" of the target; the number of models set up in the new unit is equal to the number of mortal wounds inflicted.

KEYWORDS CHAOS, MORTAL, TZEENTCH, ARCANITE, HERO, WIZARD, OGROID THAUMATURGE

TZAANGORS

Tzaangors are savage, avian beastmen dedicated to Tzeentch and gifted with his dark blessings. Shrieking and emitting shrill war calls, the Tzaangors fall upon the foe in a flurried rush of blades and vicious stabs from horns or beaks. Eager to impress their duplicitous god, the Tzaangors fight with lunatic energies, hoping to earn further gifts of change.

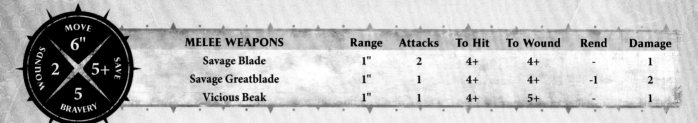

MELEE WEAPONS	Range	Attacks	To Hit	To Wound	Rend	Damage
Savage Blade	1"	2	4+	4+	-	1
Savage Greatblade	1"	1	4+	4+	-1	2
Vicious Beak	1"	1	4+	5+	-	1

MOVE 6"
WOUNDS 2
SAVE 5+
BRAVERY 5

DESCRIPTION

A unit of Tzaangors has 5 or more models. Each unit fights with a variety of weapons; some of the Tzaangors are armed with Paired Savage Blades, whilst others carry a Savage Blade and Arcanite Shield. Two in every five models in the unit can be armed with double-handed Savage Greatblades. No matter what they carry in their hands, all can also tear at the foe with their Vicious Beaks.

TWISTBRAY

The leader of this unit is a Twistbray. You can add 1 to hit rolls made for a Twistbray.

TZAANGOR MUTANT

One in every five Tzaangors can be a Tzaangor Mutant armed with Paired Savage Blades. Tzaangor Mutants make 3 attacks with their Paired Savage Blades rather than 2.

ICON BEARERS

Models in this unit may be Icon Bearers. If this unit includes one or more Icon Bearers, then at the start of each of your hero phases, take a dice for each **WIZARD** (friend or foe) within 9" of this unit. Then, pick an enemy unit within 18" and roll the dice; the unit suffers a mortal wound for each roll of 4 or more.

BRAYHORNS

Models in this unit may have a Brayhorn. A unit that includes any Brayhorns can run and charge in the same turn.

ABILITIES

Arcanite Shield: Roll a dice before allocating a wound or mortal wound to a model that has an Arcanite Shield. On a roll of 6, the shield deflects the damage and the wound is ignored.

Anarchy and Mayhem: If this unit is within 9" of any friendly **ARCANITE HEROES** at the start of the combat phase, you can add 1 to any wound rolls made for the unit in that phase.

Paired Savage Blades: You can add 1 to any hit rolls made for models attacking with Paired Savage Blades.

Savagery Unleashed: You can make one additional attack for each model in this unit with its Savage Blade, Two Savage Blades or Savage Greatblade for every 9 models in the unit (to a maximum of 3 additional attacks per model).

KEYWORDS CHAOS, GOR, TZEENTCH, ARCANITE, TZAANGORS

KAIRIC ACOLYTES

The Chanters of Change, the Kairic Acolytes are the chosen human cultists of Tzeentch. They are able to harness their collective magical might, unleashing it in the form of searing bolts. Covert in nature, many Acolytes only reveal themselves when the time to strike has come. Those enemies that do not fall before the fusillade of arcane bolts must then face the curved blades of the Acolytes.

MISSILE WEAPONS	Range	Attacks	To Hit	To Wound	Rend	Damage
Sorcerous Bolt	12"	1	5+	4+	-	1
MELEE WEAPONS	Range	Attacks	To Hit	To Wound	Rend	Damage
Cursed Blade	1"	1	4+	4+	-	1
Cursed Glaive	1"	1	4+	4+	-1	1

MOVE 6"
WOUNDS 1
SAVE 6+
BRAVERY 5

DESCRIPTION

A unit of Kairic Acolytes has 10 or more models. Each unit fights with a variety of weapons; some of the Acolytes are armed with a single Cursed Blade while others carry Paired Cursed Blades. Some instead carry a Cursed Blade and an Arcanite Shield. Three in every ten models in the unit can be armed with double-handed Cursed Glaives. All Kairic Acolytes can hurl Sorcerous Bolts.

KAIRIC ADEPT

The leader of this unit is a Kairic Adept. A Kairic Adept makes 2 attacks rather than 1 with his Sorcerous Bolt.

ABILITIES

Arcanite Shield: Roll a dice before allocating a wound or mortal wound to a model that has an Arcanite Shield. On a roll of 6, the shield deflects the damage and the wound is ignored.

Gestalt Sorcery: You can add 1 to the hit rolls of this unit's Sorcerous Bolts if it is within 9" of at least one friendly **Tzeentch Wizard**.

Paired Cursed Blades: You can add 1 to any hit rolls made for models attacking with Paired Cursed Blades.

Scroll of Dark Arts: One in ten models in the unit may carry a Scroll of Dark Arts. If at least one model in the unit is equipped with a Scroll of Dark Arts, you can increase the range of the unit's Sorcerous Bolts to 18".

Vulcharc: One in ten models in the unit may be accompanied by a Vulcharc. If at least one model in the unit is equipped with a Vulcharc, roll a dice each time an enemy **Wizard** within 18" of the unit successfully casts a spell. On a roll of 5 or more, the wizard suffers one mortal wound as soon as the spell's effects have been resolved.

KEYWORDS	CHAOS, MORTAL, TZEENTCH, ARCANITE, KAIRIC ACOLYTES

TZAANGOR ENLIGHTENED

Tzeentch's favour is highly evident upon these elite Tzaangors, for they possess strange feathers and elaborate horns, and wield ornate spears of a quality beyond the weaponry of their lesser kin. Some ride upon Discs of Tzeentch, and all can see strands of the past. Many foes are terrified as the Enlightened give voice to events from their lives that no one ought to have knowledge of.

MELEE WEAPONS	Range	Attacks	To Hit	To Wound	Rend	Damage
Tzeentchian Spear	2"	2	4+	3+	-1	2
Vicious Beak	1"	1	4+	5+	-	1
Disc of Tzeentch's Teeth and Horns	1"	D3	4+	3+	-1	D3

DESCRIPTION
A unit of Tzaangor Enlightened has 3 or more models. Each Tzaangor Enlightened is equipped with an ornate Tzeentchian Spear which it uses to skewer its foes, but can also tear at them with its Vicious Beak.

AVIARCH
The leader of this unit is an Aviarch. An Aviarch makes 3 attacks rather than 2 with its Tzeentchian Spear.

DISCS OF TZEENTCH
All models in a Tzaangor Enlightened unit can be mounted on a Disc of Tzeentch, granting them a Move of 16" and the Teeth and Horns attack. In addition, Tzaangor Enlightened on Discs of Tzeentch can fly and have a Wounds characteristic of 4 instead of 3. Furthermore, Tzaangor Enlightened on Discs of Tzeentch gain the **DAEMON** keyword.

ABILITIES
Babbling Stream of Secrets: If an enemy unit within 9" of any Tzaangor Enlightened models fails a battleshock test, one additional model flees.

Guided by the Past: In the combat phase, you can re-roll all failed hit and wound rolls for a unit of Tzaangor Enlightened if there are any enemy units within 3" of them that have already attacked in that phase.

Preternatural Enhancement: If this unit is within 9" of a Tzaangor Shaman at the start of the combat phase, add 1 to all hit rolls you make for their Tzeentchian Spear and Vicious Beak attacks.

KEYWORDS	CHAOS, GOR, TZEENTCH, ARCANITE, TZAANGOR ENLIGHTENED

TZAANGOR SKYFIRES

Atop weird Discs of Tzeentch the Tzaangor Skyfires soar across the battlefield into positions where they can rain death upon the foe. Able to catch glimpses of the future, the Skyfires send their Arrows of Fate on what appear to be baffling trajectories to an observer, but the missiles instead strike their targets' most vulnerable weak spots with confounding accuracy.

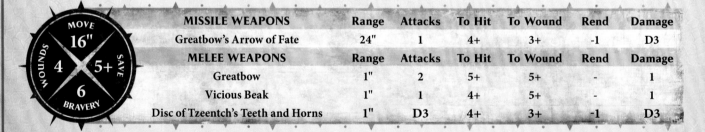

MISSILE WEAPONS	Range	Attacks	To Hit	To Wound	Rend	Damage
Greatbow's Arrow of Fate	24"	1	4+	3+	-1	D3
MELEE WEAPONS	**Range**	**Attacks**	**To Hit**	**To Wound**	**Rend**	**Damage**
Greatbow	1"	2	5+	5+	-	1
Vicious Beak	1"	1	4+	5+	-	1
Disc of Tzeentch's Teeth and Horns	1"	D3	4+	3+	-1	D3

DESCRIPTION
A unit of Tzaangor Skyfires has 3 or more models. Each Tzaangor Skyfire prefers to loose Arrows of Fate with their Greatbows from afar, but will readily savage their foes with their Vicious Beaks and club them with their Great Bows. They ride scintillating Discs of Tzeentch, the better to sight their prey; the daemonic steeds attack with piercing Teeth and Horns.

AVIARCH
The leader of this unit is an Aviarch. An Aviarch has a To Hit characteristic of 3+ instead of 4+ when firing its Greatbow's Arrow of Fate.

FLY
Tzaangor Skyfires can fly.

ABILITIES
Guided by the Future: In the combat phase, you can re-roll all failed hit and wound rolls for a unit of Tzaangor Skyfires if no enemy units within 3" of them have attacked yet in that phase.

Judgement from Afar: To be struck by an Arrow of Fate is to be judged by destiny itself. Those found wanting are all but doomed. If the hit roll for a Greatbow's Arrow of Fate is a 6 or more, the attack sequence ends and the target immediately suffers D3 mortal wounds.

Preternatural Enhancement: If this unit is within 9" of a friendly Tzaangor Shaman at the start of the shooting phase, add 1 to any hit rolls made for their Greatbow's Arrow of Fate attacks.

KEYWORDS	CHAOS, GOR, DAEMON, TZEENTCH, ARCANITE, TZAANGOR SKYFIRES

CHAOS SPAWN

The Chaos Spawn that accompany the Arcanite Cults are, if anything, even more horrifically mutated than others of their kind. Each of these creatures has been horribly altered at the whim of the Great Mutator, and instinctively shuffles, crawls or bounds towards its prey to tear them limb from limb with its freakish array of claws, tentacles and hooked appendages.

MOVE 2D6"
WOUNDS 5
SAVE 5+
BRAVERY 10

MELEE WEAPONS	Range	Attacks	To Hit	To Wound	Rend	Damage
Freakish Mutations	1"	2D6	4+	4+	-	1

DESCRIPTION

A unit of Chaos Spawn has any number of models. They are armed with a variety of Freakish Mutations.

ABILITIES

Writhing Tentacles: If you roll a double when determining the number of attacks made by a Chaos Spawn's Freakish Mutations, resolve those attacks with a To Hit and To Wound characteristic of 3+ instead of 4+.

KEYWORDS CHAOS, MORTAL, TZEENTCH, SLAVES TO DARKNESS, CHAOS SPAWN

THE RULES

Warhammer Age of Sigmar puts you in command of a force of mighty warriors, monsters and war engines. This rules sheet contains everything you need to know in order to do battle amid strange and sorcerous realms, to unleash powerful magic, darken the skies with arrows, and crush your enemies in bloody combat!

THE ARMIES

Before the conflict begins, rival warlords gather their most powerful warriors.

In order to play, you must first muster your army from the miniatures in your collection. Armies can be as big as you like, and you can use as many models from your collection as you wish. The more units you decide to use, the longer the game will last and the more exciting it will be! Typically, a game with around a hundred miniatures per side will last for about an evening.

WARSCROLLS & UNITS

All models are described by warscrolls, which provide all of the rules for using them in the game. You will need warscrolls for the models you want to use.

Models fight in units. A unit can have one or more models, but cannot include models that use different warscrolls. A unit must be set up and finish any sort of move as a single group of models, with all models within 1" of at least one other model from their unit. If anything causes a unit to become split up during a battle, it must reform the next time that it moves.

TOOLS OF WAR

In order to fight a battle you will require a tape measure and some dice.

Distances in *Warhammer Age of Sigmar* are measured in inches ("), between the closest points of the models or units you're measuring to and from. You can measure distances whenever you wish. A model's base isn't considered part of the model – it's just there to help the model stand up – so don't include it when measuring distances.

Warhammer Age of Sigmar uses six-sided dice (sometimes abbreviated to D6). If a rule requires you to roll a D3, roll a dice and halve the total, rounding fractions up. Some rules allow you to re-roll a dice roll, which means you get to roll some or all of the dice again. You can never re-roll a dice more than once, and re-rolls happen before modifiers to the roll (if any) are applied.

THE BATTLEFIELD

Be they pillars of flame, altars of brass or haunted ruins, the realms are filled with strange sights and deadly obstacles.

Battles in *Warhammer Age of Sigmar* are fought across an infinite variety of exciting landscapes in the Mortal Realms, from desolate volcanic plains and treacherous sky temples, to lush jungles and cyclopean ruins. The dominion of Chaos is all-pervading, and no land is left untouched by the blight of war. These wildly fantastical landscapes are recreated whenever you play a game of *Warhammer Age of Sigmar*.

The table and scenery you use constitute your battlefield. A battlefield can be any flat surface upon which the models can stand – for example a dining table or the floor – and can be any size or shape provided it's bigger than 3 feet square.

First you should decide in which of the seven Mortal Realms the battle will take place. For example, you might decide that your battle will take place in the Realm of Fire. Sometimes you'll need to know this in order to use certain abilities. If you can't agree on the realm, roll a dice, and whoever rolls highest decides.

The best battles are fought over lavishly designed and constructed landscapes, but whether you have a lot of scenery or only a small number of features doesn't matter! A good guide is at least 1 feature for every 2 foot square, but less is okay and more can make for a really interesting battle.

To help you decide the placement of your scenery, you can choose to roll two dice and add them together for each 2 foot square area of your battlefield and consult the following table:

Roll	Terrain Features
2-3	No terrain features.
4-5	2 terrain features.
6-8	1 terrain feature.
9-10	2 terrain features.
11-12	Choose from 0 to 3 terrain features.

MYSTERIOUS LANDSCAPES

The landscapes of the Mortal Realms can both aid and hinder your warriors. Unless stated otherwise, a model can be moved across scenery but not through it (so you can't move through a solid wall, or pass through a tree, but can choose to have a model climb up or over them). In addition, once you have set up all your scenery, either roll a dice on the following table or pick a rule from it for each terrain feature:

THE SCENERY TABLE

Roll   Scenery

1   Damned: If any of your units are within 3" of this terrain feature in your hero phase, you can declare that one is making a sacrifice. If you do so, the unit suffers D3 mortal wounds, but you can add 1 to all hit rolls for the unit until your next hero phase.

2   Arcane: Add 1 to the result of any casting or unbinding rolls made for a wizard within 3" of this terrain feature.

3   Inspiring: Add 1 to the Bravery of all units within 3" of this terrain feature.

4   Deadly: Roll a dice for any model that makes a run or charge move across, or finishing on, this terrain feature. On a roll of 1 the model is slain.

5   Mystical: Roll a dice in your hero phase for each of your units within 3" of this terrain feature. On a roll of 1 the unit is befuddled and can't be selected to cast spells, move or attack until your next hero phase. On a roll of 2-6 the unit is ensorcelled, and you can re-roll failed wound rolls for the unit until your next hero phase.

6   Sinister: Any of your units that are within 3" of this terrain feature in your hero phase cause fear until your next hero phase. Subtract 1 from the Bravery of any enemy units that are within 3" of one or more units that cause fear.

THE BATTLE BEGINS

Thunder rumbles high above as the armies take to the battlefield.

You are now ready for the battle to begin, but before it does you must set up your armies for the coming conflict.

SET-UP

Before setting up their armies, both players roll a dice, rolling again in the case of a tie. The player that rolls higher must divide the battlefield into two equal-sized halves; their opponent then picks one half to be their territory. Some examples of this are shown below.

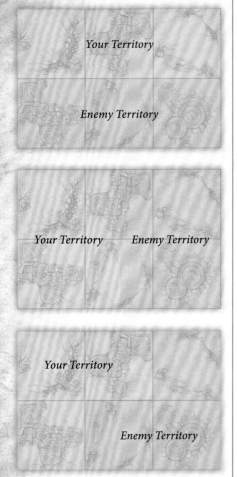

The players then alternate setting up units, one at a time, starting with the player that won the earlier dice roll. Models must be set up in their own territory, more than 12" from enemy territory.

You can continue setting up units until you have set up all the units you want to fight in this battle, or have run out of space. This is your army. Count the number of models in your army – this may come in useful later. Any remaining units are held in reserve, playing no part unless fate lends a hand.

The opposing player can continue to set up units. When they have finished, set-up is complete. The player that finishes setting up first always chooses who takes the first turn in the first battle round.

THE GENERAL

Once you have finished setting up all of your units, nominate one of the models you set up as your general. Your general has a command ability, as described in the rules for the hero phase on the next page.

GLORIOUS VICTORY

In the Mortal Realms battles are brutal and uncompromising – they are fought to the bitter end, with one side able to claim victory because it has destroyed its foe or there are no enemy models left on the field of battle. The victor can immediately claim a **major victory** and the honours and triumphs that are due to them, while the defeated must repair to their lair to lick their wounds and bear the shame of failure.

If it has not been possible to fight a battle to its conclusion or the outcome is not obvious, then a result of sorts can be calculated by comparing the number of models removed from play with the number of models originally set up for the battle for each army. Expressing these as percentages provides a simple way to determine the winner. Such a victory can only be claimed as a **minor victory**. For example, if one player lost 75% of their starting models, and the other player lost 50%, then the player that only lost 50% of their models could claim a minor victory.

Models added to your army during the game (for example, through summoning, reinforcements, reincarnation and so on) do not count towards the number of models in the army, but must be counted among the casualties an army suffers.

SUDDEN DEATH VICTORIES

Sometimes a player may attempt to achieve a sudden death victory. If one army has a third more models than the other, the outnumbered player can choose one objective from the sudden death table after generals are nominated. A **major victory** can be claimed immediately when the objective is achieved by the outnumbered player.

TRIUMPHS

After any sudden death objectives have been chosen, if your army won a major victory in its previous battle, roll a dice and look up the result on the triumph table to the right.

THE SUDDEN DEATH TABLE

Assassinate: The enemy player picks a unit with the **Hero**, **Wizard**, **Priest** or **Monster** keyword in their army. Slay the unit that they pick.
Blunt: The enemy player picks a unit with five or more models in their army. Slay the unit that they pick.
Endure: Have at least one model which started the battle on the battlefield still in play at the end of the sixth battle round.
Seize Ground: Pick one terrain feature in enemy territory. Have at least one friendly model within 3" of that feature at the end of the fourth battle round.

THE TRIUMPH TABLE

Roll	Triumph
1-2	**Blessed:** You can change the result of a single dice to the result of your choosing once during the battle.
3-4	**Inspired:** You can re-roll all of the failed hit rolls for one unit in your army in one combat phase.
5-6	**Empowered:** Add 1 to your general's Wounds characteristic.

BATTLE ROUNDS

Mighty armies crash together amid the spray of blood and the crackle of magic.

Warhammer Age of Sigmar is played in a series of battle rounds, each of which is split into two turns – one for each player. At the start of each battle round, both players roll a dice, rolling again in the case of a tie. The player that rolls highest decides who takes the first turn in that battle round. Each turn consists of the following phases:

1. *Hero Phase*
   Cast spells and use heroic abilities.
2. *Movement Phase*
   Move units across the battlefield.
3. *Shooting Phase*
   Attack with missile weapons.
4. *Charge Phase*
   Charge units into combat.
5. *Combat Phase*
   Pile in and attack with melee weapons.
6. *Battleshock Phase*
   Test the bravery of depleted units.

Once the first player has finished their turn, the second player takes theirs. Once the second player has also finished, the battle round is over and a new one begins.

PRE-BATTLE ABILITIES

Some warscrolls allow you to use an ability 'after set-up is complete'. These abilities are used before the first battle round. If both armies have abilities like this, both players roll a dice, re-rolling in the case of a tie. The player that rolls highest gets to use their abilities first, followed by their opponent.

HERO PHASE

As the armies close in, their leaders use sorcerous abilities, make sacrifices to the gods, or give strident commands.

In your hero phase you can use the wizards in your army to cast spells (see the rules for wizards on the last page of these rules).

In addition, other units in your army may have abilities on their warscrolls that can be used in the hero phase. Generally, these can only be used in your own hero phase. However, if an ability says it can be used in every hero phase, then it can be used in your opponent's hero phase as well as your own. If both players can use abilities in a hero phase, the player whose turn it is gets to use all of theirs first.

COMMAND ABILITY

In your hero phase, your general can use one command ability. All generals have the Inspiring Presence command ability, and some may have more on their warscroll.

Inspiring Presence: Pick a unit from your army that is within 12" of your general. The unit that you pick does not have to take battleshock tests until your next hero phase.

MOVEMENT PHASE

The ground shakes to the tread of marching feet as armies vie for position.

Start your movement phase by picking one of your units and moving each model in that unit until you've moved all the models you want to. You can then pick another unit to move, until you have moved as many of your units as you wish. No model can be moved more than once in each movement phase.

MOVING

A model can be moved in any direction, to a distance in inches equal to or less than the Move characteristic on its warscroll. It can be moved vertically in order to climb or cross scenery, but cannot be moved across other models. No part of the model may move further than the model's Move characteristic.

ENEMY MODELS

When you move a model in the movement phase, you may not move within 3" of any enemy models. Models from your army are friendly models, and models from the opposing army are enemy models.

Units starting the movement phase within 3" of an enemy unit can either remain stationary or retreat. If you choose to retreat, the unit must end its move more than 3" away from all enemy units. If a unit retreats, then it can't shoot or charge later that turn (see below).

RUNNING

When you pick a unit to move in the movement phase, you can declare that it will run. Roll a dice and add the result to the Move characteristic of all models in the unit for the movement phase. A unit that runs can't shoot or charge later that turn.

FLYING

If the warscroll for a model says that the model can fly, it can pass across models and scenery as if they were not there. It still may not finish the move within 3" of an enemy in the movement phase, and if it is already within 3" of an enemy it can only retreat or remain stationary.

SHOOTING PHASE

A storm of death breaks over the battle as arrows fall like rain and war machines hurl their deadly payloads.

In your shooting phase you can shoot with models armed with missile weapons.

Pick one of your units. You may not pick a unit that ran or retreated this turn. Each model in the unit attacks with all of the missile weapons it is armed with (see Attacking). After all of the models in the unit have shot, you can choose another unit to shoot with, until all units that can shoot have done so.

CHARGE PHASE

Howling bloodcurdling war cries, warriors hurl themselves into battle to slay with blade, hammer and claw.

Any of your units within 12" of the enemy in your charge phase can make a charge move. Pick an eligible unit and roll two dice. Each model in the unit can move this number in inches. You may not pick a unit that ran or retreated this turn, nor one that is within 3" of the enemy.

The first model you move must finish within ½" of an enemy model. If that's impossible, the charge has failed and no models in the charging unit can move in this phase. Once you've moved all the models in the unit, you can pick another eligible unit to make a charge, until all units that can charge have done so.

COMBAT PHASE

Carnage engulfs the battlefield as the warring armies tear each other apart.

Any unit that has charged or has models within 3" of an enemy unit can attack with its melee weapons in the combat phase.

The player whose turn it is picks a unit to attack with, then the opposing player must attack with a unit, and so on until all eligible units on both sides have attacked once each. If one side completes all its attacks first, then the other side completes all of its remaining attacks, one unit after another. No unit can be selected to attack more than once in each combat phase. An attack is split into two steps: first the unit piles in, and then you make attacks with the models in the unit.

Step 1: When you pile in, you may move each model in the unit up to 3" towards the closest enemy model. This will allow the models in the unit to get closer to the enemy in order to attack them.

Step 2: Each model in the unit attacks with all of the melee weapons it is armed with (see Attacking).

BATTLESHOCK PHASE

Even the bravest heart may quail when the horrors of battle take their toll.

In the battleshock phase, both players must take battleshock tests for units from their army that have had models slain during the turn. The player whose turn it is tests first.

To make a battleshock test, roll a dice and add the number of models from the unit that have been slain this turn. For each point by which the total exceeds the highest Bravery characteristic in the unit, one model in that unit must flee and is removed from play. Add 1 to the Bravery characteristic being used for every 10 models that are in the unit when the test is taken.

You must choose which models flee from the units you command.